SCOTLAND'S SPORTING HEROES

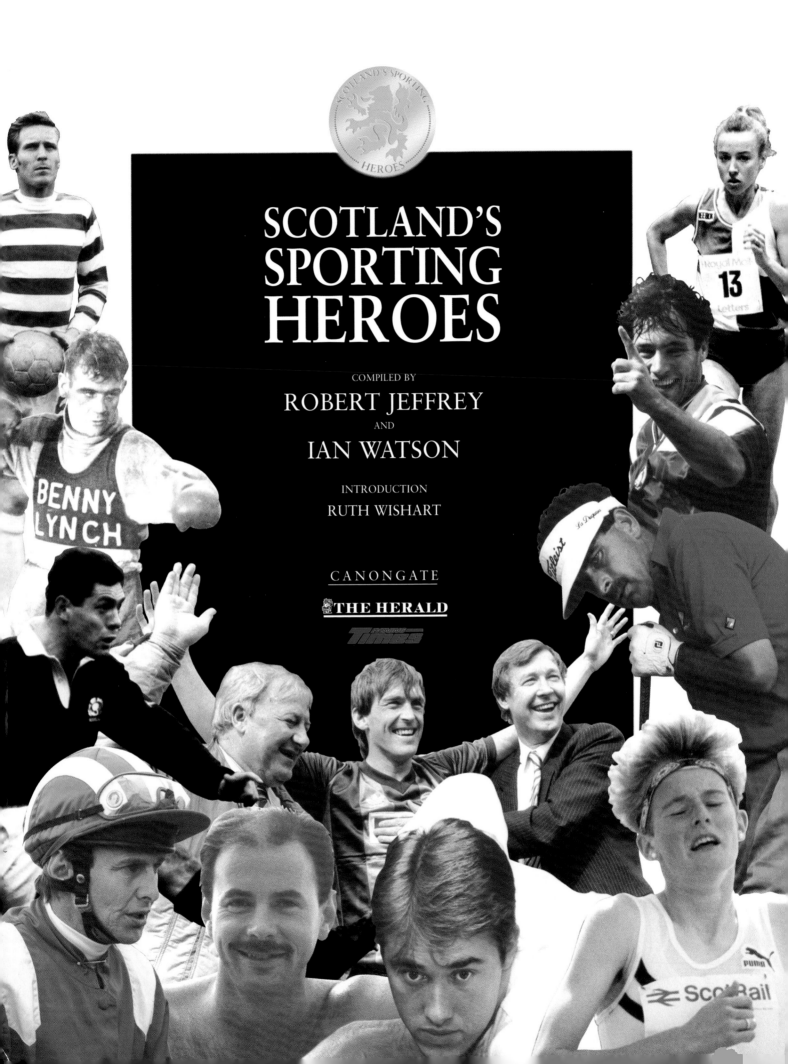

SCOTLAND'S SPORTING HEROES

COMPILED BY

ROBERT JEFFREY

AND

IAN WATSON

INTRODUCTION

RUTH WISHART

CANONGATE

THE HERALD

Evening Times

Firdt published in Great Britain in 1997 by
Canongate Books Limited,
14 High Street,
Edinburgh,
EH1 1TE

© Scottish Media Newspapers

Copies of most pictures in this book are available for personal or
commercial use.
Contact: Photo Sales Department, Scottish Media Newspapers,
195 Albion Street, Glasgow G1 1QP
quoting the picture reference number.

ACKNOWLEDGEMENTS

This book could not have been produced without the skill and
dedication of *The Herald* and *Evening Times* staff photographers down
the years. From bleak, snowy days at Murrayfield or Hampden to sun-
baked Opens at Troon, from minor athletics meetings to town hall
boxing promotions – they caught the unforgettable images of
Scotland's Heroes.

The assistance, and exhaustive sporting knowledge of the following
people in the preparation of this book is gratefully acknowledged: the
staff of *The Herald* and *Evening Times* library, Jane Westmorland, Doug
Gillon, Ken Gallacher, Ian Paul, Jim Reynolds, Mike Hildrey, Jack
Robertson, Bob Crampsey, Eddie Rodger, John Quinn, Harry McArthur,
Robert Braid, John Beattie and Jack Webster.

ISBN 0 86241 732 5

Printed in Spain by Artes Gráficas ELKAR S. Coop., 48012 Bilbao.

CONTENTS

INTRODUCTION

By Ruth Wishart

The yellow and red rosette was on her kitchen wall till the day she died. Nothing would have persuaded the late Effie Morrison to discard the memory of the day Partick Thistle had beaten the mighty Celtic in the League Cup Final. For the Scottish actress, one of the stars of the original Dr Finlay series, these were 90 magic minutes. Denis McQuade was the unlikely hero of the hour, as he remained down the years for Jags fans. No strangers to disappointment, reared on anti-climax, they had some difficulty coming to terms with the sight of the club colours fluttering from a piece of very unfamiliar silverware.

Heroes are made, they are not born, fashioned from circumstance and serendipity, like Archie Gemmill, snatching Scottish dignity from the jaws of embarrassment in Argentina, or like slim Jim Baxter, intuitively understanding the hunger of the Scots crowd for England's World Cup winning side to be humbled. Humbled 5 - 0 would have been better yet, but the one goal margin of the record books gives little indication of the heart-felt satisfaction of the tartan army that afternoon in 1967. Sometimes soccer heroes remain so in part because of their rarity value. Would the 1928 Wembley victors still have been "the wizards" of popular mythology if their immediate successors had also been victors on foreign soil? Sometimes, like Hibs' Famous Five, they represent a truly spectacular array of complementary talent. And occasionally, like the Lisbon Lions, their niche in the hall of fame is guaranteed by the sheer magnitude of their accomplishment. The mark of true respect is often a nickname which survives when its owner has long since gone to the great dressing room in the sky, or a folk ditty crooned to successive generations:

"Oh Charlie Shaw,
He nivir saw,
Where Alan Morton pit the baw."

Then there is the matter of temperament. Some great footballers have attracted adulation in spite of a personality for whom the word dour seems quite inadequate. Some seem to become effortlessly popular despite the suspicion that their skills are less legendary than they appear. Were you to compare the technical ability of a Davie Cooper or a Jinky Johnstone with Ally McCoist, you might reasonably conclude that Cooper and Johnstone were the most obviously gifted, despite McCoist's impressive goalscoring ability. Yet McCoist is unquestionably a hero, and is that rare breed of Old Firm footballer whose popularity crosses the sectarian divide.

For Scotland's rugby fraternity the last two decades have witnessed an unexpected parade of heroics for a nation whose catchment area for that sport is still woefully narrow. Gavin Hastings, all square-jawed Scottish determination, would already have been marked out as hero material by Central Casting, but what made him an icon was a moment of inspiration in Paris – the matchwinning last-second try of every schoolboy's dream. David Sole's great moment was the heart-stopping slow march on to Murrayfield which brought tears to the eyes of the most macho supporter.

For heroes, of course, you need matching villains as an essential counterpoint to the worshipping process. The English nation has served us well in this regard across team sport, but for Lynch, Keenan, McGowan, McTaggart, Buchanan, Watt and all the other lords of the boxing ring, the man in the black hat was equally easy to identify – whoever had the temerity to step up to our boy. Boxing is the sport which lends itself naturally to the pugilistic side of the Scottish character but other successes are less easily explicable. Can it be perhaps that heroes beget heroes? That the genius of Jim Clark was inspirational in the extraordinary success of Jackie Stewart, or the exploits of the latter important in the ambitions of a David Coulthard, or for that matter the dominance of the Clan McRae in rallying?

Did the emergence of Hendry persuade a generation of young men to misspend rather more of their youth in snooker halls? Or possibly, like darts, snooker is a sport with easy access, and one associated with Scotland's entrenched pub culture. Jocky Wilson, rotund, dentally challenged, ever unlikely to be confused with sex symbolism, nevertheless became an object of national regard. For, while some sports people become god-like because we know their prodigious talents to be well beyond our own abilities, men like Wilson, conversely, engage our attention because they are doing something we feel we might also do as well if we put in the hours.

Men like Richard Corsie, engaged in the profoundly unglamorous sport of bowls, attract the same slightly back-handed form of compliment from their public. His achievements are light years from ours, but that doesn't prevent the well-entrenched, if risible, belief that only practice time separates them. This is less true of other mass participation sports like golf. Only the most deluded Saturday four ball hacker would conclude that they are but a few lessons away from picking up a Masters jacket as worn by Sandy Lyle. But the ability to identify, however crudely, with the making of great golf shots does mean that the passion and the triumphs are shared. It even helps if the top of the Scottish leader board is peopled by those whose characters are less than flawless, as witness the immense support for men like Torrance and Montgomerie – never more fervently supported then when they have once more dropped a winning script.

It is only on occasions like the making of this book, when the exhaustive picture archives of *The Herald* and *Evening Times* have been ruthlessly plundered, that you realise just how very many wonderful sporting memories this tiny nation has been privileged to enjoy. Many of you will recall that dripping wet Saturday afternoon in 1970 when two men called Stewart successively won gold for Scotland at the Commonwealth Games. Or the sight of a victorious Yvonne Murray wrapped in the Saltire or McColgan breasting a tape in front of the world's finest.

We all have special memories we recall, and, inevitably, we all rate those personal highlights in different order. That is why this book has no pretensions to being an all-inclusive list of Scottish achievement or in any sense an encyclopaedia of sport. Like all such publications it is the product of the subjective judgement of those who pretend that it is hard work to sift through a treasure trove of magical moments. The dictionary tells us that a hero is someone admired for the exceptional quality of their achievements. This book is full of achievements of quite exceptional quality. But it also recalls moments of defeat as well as glory, moments of tragedy as well as triumph. When the players and the performers are all Scottish, how could it be otherwise?

Ruth Wishart is a columnist and broadcaster and member of several different divisions of tartan armies.

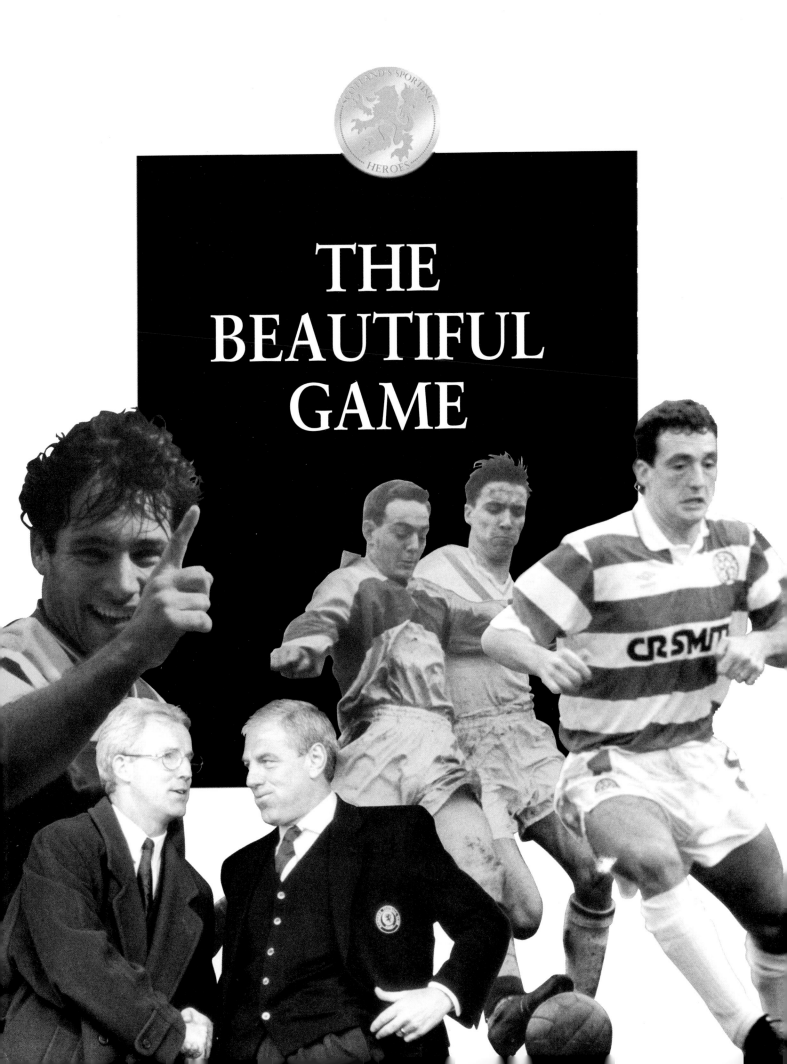

THE
BEAUTIFUL
GAME

SHF 1

SHF 2

ALEX JAMES

Perhaps the most famous pair of baggy shorts in football! Alex James was arguably the greatest football genius of his day. He won only eight Scottish caps because of various fall outs with the selectors, a tradition that has been carried forward to this day. From Mossend in Lanarkshire, his Arsenal heyday was the early 30s.

ALAN MORTON

Rangers' legendary left-winger, famous for his speed and ability to float crosses into the goal mouth. His Rangers team mate Alex Jackson scored a hat trick in the famous Wembley Wizards victory over England in 1928 – all of the goals coming from Morton crosses. His following was so great that at the height of his fame the rhyme "Oh Charlie Shaw, He nivir saw, Where Alan Morton pit the baw" was on everyone's lips. He was a mining engineer who played 495 games for Rangers despite being a part-time professional. He later became a member of the board.

SHF 3

HUGHIE GALLACHER

Standing at only 5ft 2in, Gallacher was a prodigious goal scorer, frequently with his head. Many reckon him Scotland's greatest centre forward, even though he did not score in the Wembley Wizards' 5–1 thrashing of England in 1928. His superb ball skills thrilled the fans of many British clubs including Airdrie and Newcastle, but sadly for Gallacher the price of fame was high. After a battle with alcohol and amid domestic strife, he took his own life under the wheels of a train.

JOHN THOMSON (opposite page)

A shot taken on a tragic afternoon in Scotland's football history, when Celtic goalkeeper John Thomson died after an accidental collision with Rangers forward Sam English in September 1931. This poignant photograph, taken shortly before the accident, shows Thomson, who was lauded for his bravery and considered by many to be the best keeper of his time, taking out a cross with Sam English in the foreground. Thousands of mourners walked from Glasgow to Thomson's home village of Cardenden in Fife for the funeral.

SHF 5

SHF 4

SCOT SYMON AND WILLIE LYON

Scot Symon, here shaking hands with Celtic skipper Willie Lyon on a snowy Ibrox before the start of an Old Firm battle, went on to become one of Rangers' most successful managers. On another occasion, when fog rather than snow was the problem, Symon the manager made one of his famous quotations. When asked about the likelihood of the game proceeding, he replied, "I don't know and don't quote me".

JIMMY McGRORY

Celtic's Jimmy McGrory had an amazing scoring record. In a career of 400 games he averaged more than a goal a game, the sort of record that would make him multi-million pound transfer material these days. His peak was in the 30s when hat tricks were his speciality and he clocked up five goals in one game against Aberdeen, four against St Mirren and three in three minutes against Motherwell. He later became manager of Celtic.

SHF 9

PATSY GALLAGHER

Patsy Gallagher was one of the old-time Celtic greats with real star quality. A skillful and mischievous player, he scored a marvellous winning goal in the 1925 Cup Final against Dundee. The mischief in his character was evinced on an occasion when he dressed up as an old lady to break out of training. Celtic's Sir Robert Kelly thought Patsy the greatest of them all.

SHF 6

TOMMY MUIRHEAD

Muirhead joined Rangers in 1917 and graced the team either as wing half or inside forward until 1930, apart from a brief spell in the USA as player/manager of Boston. He captained Rangers and won five League Championship medals, and although he did not play in the 1928 final he was awarded a winner's medal. After a brief spell in management, he followed what has become a well-worn path into sports journalism. He died in 1979 aged 82.

SHF 7

JIMMY DELANEY

A speedy right-winger whose career extended from 1933 to 1957 playing with Celtic, Manchester United, Aberdeen, Derry City, Cork Athletic and Elgin City, Delaney is unique in having won Cup Winners' medals in England, Scotland and Ireland. Here he is in the early 50s playing for Aberdeen.

SHF 12

SHF 10

SHF 8

JIMMY MASON

Jimmy Mason, perhaps the biggest star of all for the now defunct Third Lanark. He had a few caps in the late 40s and early 50s but his genius built him a huge following among Third Lanark fans at Cathkin Park.

JERRY DAWSON

One of the most famous Rangers keepers, Jerry Dawson has fond memories of the early days of touring. "We went by boat, we had time to see the country, we lived like lords and the opposition were pushovers." Modern heroes, facing a hasty flight and a tough match, might not envy the £15 per week he earned but might enjoy the less hectic schedule.

DAVIE MEIKLEJOHN

Reckoned to be one of Rangers' greatest ever players and captains, 'Meek' was anything but that. A determined and inspirational right-half, he led the Ibrox club to five League Championships in a row between 1927 and 1931 and his goal from the penalty spot in the 1928 Cup Final against Celtic paved the way for Rangers to lift the trophy for the first time in 25 years. He played for and captained Scotland as well as enjoying a spell as manager of Partick Thistle, a career move followed by many an Ibrox favourite over the years.

TORRY GILLICK

Gillick was a player of mercurial talent, of the kind managers have to allow a little more latitude than other mortals. Astoundingly fast over 5–10 yards, only Jimmy Greaves was anything like as quick off the mark. In a 1945 game against the famous Moscow Dynamo, Rangers may just have been able to win were it not for the fact the Russian XI was not an XI at all for at least part of the game. Gillick, bemused at his team's defence being quite so overstretched, finally remarked to a team-mate. "Thae commies huv goat twelve players oan the park". And so they had! Torry is shown here guesting for Partick Thistle during the war.

SHF 13

WILLIE McNAUGHT

A typically gritty action shot of Willie McNaught of Raith Rovers who won five caps for Scotland in the 50s. He was another graphic example of a European class player who missed out on the big cheques of today.

SHF 14

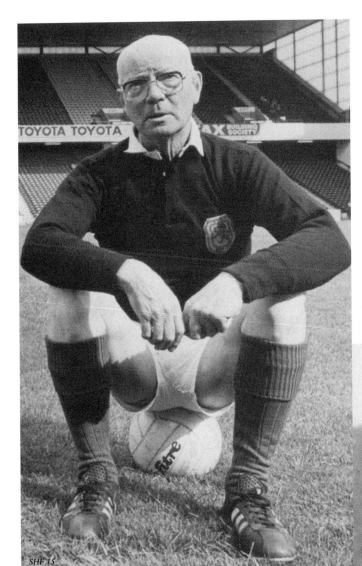

SHF 15

BOB McPHAIL

One of the footballing legends of the Roaring Twenties, Bob McPhail won his first Scottish Cup medal at the age of 19 playing for the finest Airdrieonian team of all time. He would gain greater prominence when he joined Rangers to partner that other legend of Ibrox, Alan Morton. But he had always maintained that that Airdrie team, which included yet another legend in the wayward genius of Hughie Gallacher, was worthy of comparison with any of the Rangers formations in which he subsequently played. Rangers had not won the Scottish Cup for 25 years before his arrival, but he proceeded to add six Cup medals to his Airdrie one – and to claim his part in nine League Championships. Life for the football stars of that era was radically different from today. McPhail recalls travelling to play Hearts when manager Bill Struth would take his team off the train at Haymarket and walk them smartly to Tynecastle. They were all decked out in bowler hats and white collars, blue suits and blue overcoats with velvet collars, black socks and black shoes. No one dared step out of line. McPhail is shown here in the modern setting of Ibrox.

SHF 16

JIMMY CARABINE

Jimmy Carabine was one of the most famous of Third Lanark's pre-war stars, a man whose career was blighted by the war. After his playing career he became a well-known sports writer.

SHF 18

TOMMY WALKER

One of the great footballers of the 30s, Walker went on to become one of Hearts' most successful managers. He served the club for more than 50 years, finally as Vice-Chairman. An extremely stylish and effective player, he was first capped in 1935. Here, along side George Graham former S.F.A. secretary, he makes a charity appeal to the crowd at a war-time army international between Scotland and England. Such games attracted huge crowds in entertainment-starved wartime.

WILLIE BAULD

The shorts were getting shorter but goalies still wore the bright yellow woolly jersey as sported by Rangers' George Niven in this mid 50s shot which also features two legendary Hearts players, Jimmy Wardhaugh, left, and Willie Bauld, centre, who with Alfie Conn senior were known as the 'Terrible Trio'.

WILLIE WADDELL (opposite page)

Impressive physically, Willie Waddell or 'The Deedle', seen here in full flow as a player, was a hugely entertaining and effective player for Rangers and Scotland whose international career lasted into the 50s. He also became one of the most successful managers in the club's history, and had a very successful career as a journalist before the remarkable feat of winning the League with Kilmarnock and then returning to his first love, Rangers. He pioneered modern stadiums for Scotland after building an impressive new Ibrox in the 70s, long before the all-seater requirements.

SHF 20

SHF 19

MATT BUSBY

Like many of the world's greatest football managers, Busby's playing career was eclipsed by his later successes. His resilience in overcoming the tragedy of the Munich air crash in 1958 to steer Manchester United to victory in the European Cup ten years later made him a cornerstone of sporting history. From Bellshill, Busby's name will always be linked with his Busby 'Babes', many of whom died in the air crash. He was knighted in 1968. In this evocative shot, probably from a war-time international, he leads out Scotland against an English side captained by Joe Mercer.

SHF 21

WILLIE WOODBURN

Rangers heroes tend to be renowned for their strength and stamina. None more so than Willie Woodburn, seen here with Celtic's Willie Fernie. Signed for Rangers in 1937, he played until he was suspended *sine die* in 1954 after being sent off against Stirling Albion. The ban, which followed an alleged kick at an opponent, took account of his record of indiscipline, but, while it was rescinded after two years, Woodburn did not return to playing. He played in some the great games of the late 40s early 50s, including the 1953 Scottish Cup Final against Aberdeen which Rangers won 1–0 in front of a crowd of 113,000!

BOBBY BROWN

Bobby Brown in action for Rangers against Hearts at Tynecastle. Brown went on to manage Scotland in the early 60s when, at one stage, Ibrox men John Greig, Ronnie McKinnon, Dave Smith and Willie Mathieson all played for him.

SHF 22

SHF 23

GEORGE HAMILTON

Even if distance lends enchantment, George Hamilton still emerges as a golden memory for Aberdonians. Rejected by Rangers, he went to Pittodrie via Queen of the South in 1938, but was part of that generation severely harmed by the war. Remembered for his promise, Hamilton was given a hero's welcome home in 1945 that set the scene for the post-war triumphs – Aberdeen's first-ever trophy (League Cup in 1946), first Scottish Cup in 1947 and first League Championship, in 1955. Hamilton, who had partnered the great Tom Finney in the Army team, was known for his balletic beauty of movement, inch-perfect passing and the best heading of a ball Pittodrie has ever seen. Though 'Gentleman George' could look after himself, he was booked only once in 18 years at the top – for saying "I don't think that was a foul, ref"!

GEORGE YOUNG

Nicknamed 'Corky' because he always carried a lucky champagne cork, Young first played for Rangers in 1941. Although 6ft 2in and 15 stones, he was renowned for his gentleness and kindness. In 701 first team games for Rangers and 53 for Scotland, Young was booked only once – and that was for speaking up in defence of a team-mate. A giant of a man, he is seen here towering over his Scottish teammates.

SHF 24

SHF 25

JIMMY COWAN

Morton's Jimmy Cowan was famous for his cat-like leaps and on many occasions rescued Scotland when under pressure. He enjoyed his heyday in the early 50s and went on to win 25 caps.

SHF 28

DAVE MacKAY

Despite two leg breaks in his career, Dave Mackay still managed 22 international caps for Scotland, although his admirers thought that the figure should have been even more. With Hearts he won a full set of Scottish medals – League Cup, League and the Scottish Cup in the mid 50s. He added to his medal collection with Spurs, where he was skipper, before moving to Derby County. While there he was named joint Footballer of the Year. A hard tackling half-back of the old school, he went on to manage Derby and Birmingham City, amongst other clubs, and had a spell as coach in the Middle East. He managed Derby's Championship winning side of the mid 70s.

THE FAMOUS FIVE

This is Hibs' legendary forward line of the 50s as it started out. Scratch a fan and ask them who the Famous Five were and the answer is Gordon Smith, Eddie Turnbull, Laurie Reilly, Bobby Johnstone and Willie Ormond. Ask any slightly older fan and you get this answer – Smith, Turnbull, Reilly, Bobby Coombe and Ormond, as in this picture. Coombe dropped back to be a midfielder as the Hibs team of that era developed. Bobby Johnstone is inset. So perhaps it really should be the famous six!

SHF 26

SHF 27

BOBBY EVANS

A hugely energetic defender for Celtic, Evans joined the club in 1944 and in early seasons at Parkhead played inside forward before dropping back to become the centrepiece of the defence. He played in Celtic's famous Coronation Cup Final victory against Hibs in 1953 at Hampden, when more than 117,000 people were in the ground, and he was a regular for Scotland. Here he leads the team out against England at Hampden in 1960. The England captain is Bill Slater of Wolves.

TOMMY YOUNGER

A gentle giant of a man, Younger lived for Scottish football. Before he died in 1984 he was SFA President and highly regarded as an ambassador and administrator. As a goalkeeper of outstanding ability who played for Hibs, Liverpool and Leeds United, he represented his country 24 times and, unusually for a keeper, captained the side in the 1958 World Cup in Sweden.

SHF 30

SHF 31

JOE BAKER, LAWRIE REILLY AND PAT STANTON

A hat trick of Hibernian stars seen here launching the Hibs 'Hat Trick' Lottery. Thanks to the geographic accident of being born in Liverpool, Joe Baker played for England despite being Scottish through and through (the rules then were based on birthplace alone, rather than parentage). He began playing for Hibs at 16, scoring 159 goals in his first four seasons. With Denis Law he sampled Italian football with Torino, where he was seldom paid his full fortune of £100 a week because of the Italian penchant for fining players for things like missing chances or not playing well. A serious car accident nearly ended his career but remarkably he bounced back to become a top scorer with Arsenal. Later in his career he spent a miserable year at Sunderland, enlivened only by 'crazy' Jim Baxter.

A member of the celebrated Famous Five forward line, Lawrie 'Last

Minute' Reilly savours the time he beat Alf Ramsay to the ball to hammer home Scotland's equaliser in the dying seconds against England at Wembley in 1953. Of the 7–2 defeat by the Auld Enemy two years later, he remembers the team played well "except for ...ne elementary mistakes at the back", proof surely of a distant relationship to Brazil.

Pat Stanton, a player of great poise and style, became without doubt the most important Hibs player since the phenomenon of the Famous Five. Records may not tell lies, but they can fall short of the truth: this outstanding performer and ambassador for the game made only 16 appearances for his country. He later went on to play for Celtic, picking up a League Championship and Scottish Cup medals. A managerial career with several clubs eventually took him back to Easter Road as Bertie Auld's assistant.

SHF 33

IAN ST. JOHN

Ian St. John was a talented goal scorer both for Motherwell and Liverpool. With Motherwell he scored 79 goals in 113 League games before joining Liverpool in 1961 for £35,000. He played with Bill Shankly's team until 1971, with his brilliant header in extra time in the 1965 FA Cup Final making history by taking the cup to Anfield for the first time. After the completion of his highly successful on-field career, he made a name for himself as a TV pundit, in particular working with Jimmy Greaves in *The Saint and Greavesie* show.

SHF 32

BILLY STEEL

Billy Steel on the right, being takled by Raith Rovers' Malky McLure became a professional in 1941 and his career development was delayed by the war but he played in the first post-war match between England and Scotland in 1947. He was signed by Derby County that summer – the first five-figure fee paid by an English club to a Scottish club. He returned to Dundee in 1950 for a Scottish record fee of £23,000 and played a role in two League Cup wins and in the Scottish Cup Final of 1952. He left Scotland to play in America and eventually worked in Los Angeles in advertising.

SHF 34

FRANK HAFFEY

The hero as villian. This famous shot shows Frank Haffey haunted by the figure 9 as Scotland's goalkeeper at Wembley arrives back in Scotland after the humiliation of a 9–3 defeat at the hands of the English. Haffey's career was a classic example of how a hero in defence can suddenly find his whole career blighted by a high profile afternoon of disaster. Many a 90 minutes Haffey was a Celtic hero but Wembley 1961 was unforgettable.

SHF 35

DAVIE McPARLAND

After a distinguished playing career at Firhill, McParland wrote his place in the hall of fame as manager of the Partick Thistle team that, against all the odds, thrashed Celtic 4–1 in the 1971 League Cup Final. After that famous victory he moved to Celtic Park as Jock Stein's assistant before spells as coach with Queen's Park and Hamilton Accies. He once complained about media exaggeration of the jet-setting life style of footballers: in his 20 years at Firhill his travels took him no further than Elgin!

SHF 36

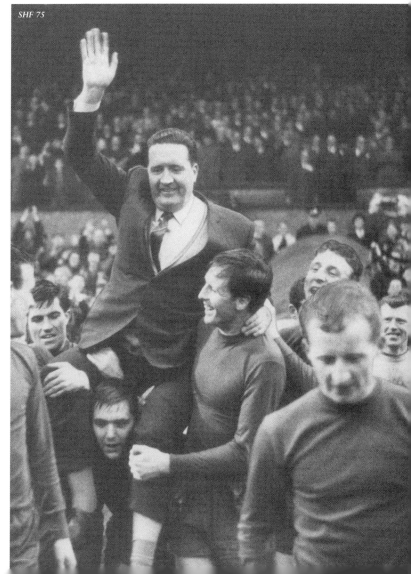

SHF 75

JOCK STEIN, BILLY McNEILL AND BILL SHANKLY

A remarkable trio. Two legendary managers, Jock Stein of Celtic and Bill Shankly of Liverpool indulge in some banter that seems to be entertaining Billy McNeill. Stein is forever a hero for blending the skills of the famous Lisbon Lions who, in 1967, became the first British team to win the European Cup. As international team manager he died of a heart attack watching Scotland hold Wales to a 1–1 draw en route to qualifying for the 1986 World Cup Finals in Mexico. Shankly, who came from Glenbuck and played for the Cherry Pickers, was one of five brothers who played professional football. He was the man who built Liverpool Football Club into one of the giants of Europe and was a king of the one-liners. After Stein's remarkable victory in Lisbon, Shankly – the only British manager to attend the game – said "You're immortal now, John".

Right, Stein is chaired onto the field by the Celtic team at the end of the 1967 season.

SHF 37

SHF 38

PAT CRERAND

Crerand started his international career at Celtic where he was a great favourite with the crowd. In 1963 he was sold to Manchester United, where his intelligent wing-half play helped United lift the Cup that year. He also played a major role in the League Championship wins in 1965 and 1967. As the photograph shows, he was a tough tackler – often in trouble with referees he was red-carded six times. His opponent is Willie Wallace then with Hearts.

BERTIE AULD

A Lisbon Lion, Auld is one of the game's larger-than-life characters whose legendary audacity inspired both his team and the crowd. Tales are legion. On a tour while manager of Partick Thistle he fell foul of his own curfew and had to throw pebbles at a player's window to get back into the hotel. As a player for Birmingham City in a match against Barcelona in the Nou Camp Stadium he said to Scots referee Tom Wharton, "Remarkable. A crowd of 100,000 and only two Scots". After a bad foul, Wharton called him over for an update on the situation: "Remarkable," he said, "100,000 and now only one Scot".

JIM BAXTER (opposite page)

An outrageous, wonderful talent. 'Slim' Jim Baxter was one of the few Scots of his time who could be termed as genuinely world class. He had many magnificent matches in the 60s both for Rangers and his country – many will remember him in 1967 dazzling and teasing World Cup holders England with a display of keepy-uppy and sitting on the ball or, four years earlier, all cockiness and coolness, sliding a penalty past Gordon Banks as if playing in a practice match rather than in front of 100,000 at Wembley.

SHF 40

SHF 39

BILLY McNEILL

One of the all time greats. A powerful, dominating centre-half with the happy knack of coming forward to score vital goals, McNeill was known by his team mates as 'Caesar'. He led by example as Celtic totally dominated the domestic scene for nearly a decade, and he had the honour of lifting the European Cup as captain of the Lisbon Lions in 1967. He returned triumphantly to Celtic as manager to lead them to a League and Cup double in 1988. After playing he enjoyed a career in management with Aberdeen, Celtic, Manchester City and Aston Villa.

JOHN GREIG

One of several contenders for the accolade of the greatest captain in the history of Rangers, Greig led the club to their first European honour, the Cup Winners' Cup in Barcelona in 1972. He was an inspirational player and captain, never giving less than 100 per cent and enjoying many magnificent battles with Jimmy Johnstone in Old Firm matches. "I used to play keepy-uppy with the wee man," he used to joke. Following his retirement in 1978 he managed Rangers until 1983 and is now the club's Public Relations Executive. In this picture he is followed onto the Ibrox turf by 'keeper Billy Ritchie in 1966

SHF 44

TOMMY GEMMELL

A swashbuckling left-back, Gemmell will always be remembered for his equalising thunderbolt against Inter Milan in the 1967 European Cup Final. Often considered an extra forward for Celtic, he scored many other vital goals and could always thrill the crowd whether in the hoops of Celtic or the blue of Scotland.

JIMMY JOHNSTONE (opposite page)

One of the best wingers ever seen on the footballing stage, Johnstone was yet another Scot with a fiery temperament to match his red hair. Had it not been for his exceptional talent it would be doubtful whether any manager would have put up with him for as long as Jock Stein did. Jock once remarked that one of his biggest achievements in football was keeping Johnstone at the top level for such a long period. Jimmy's team mates were often grateful to him for his ability to take the ball for a long walk down the right wing and relieve pressure on the defence in the dying minutes of important games. He was a specialist in leaping over hard-tackling opponents – on this occasion Jim Heriott the Hibs 'keeper.

WILLIE HENDERSON

Scotland has a knack of breeding diminutive wingers. At 5ft 4in 'Wee' Willie Henderson was prodigy, playing for Rangers at the age of 17 and for Scotland at 18. He thrilled the Ibrox fans of the 60s with his pace, control and sorties down the right wing, usually culminating in a perfectly flighted ball into the box for predators Jimmy Millar and Ralph Brand. Capped 29 times (21 of those before he was 23) he had to compete for the Scotland No 7 jersey with that other great wizard of the right wing, Celtic's Jimmy Johnstone. He is seen here beating Celtic's Jim Kennedy.

SHF 45

RONNIE SIMPSON

'Faither', the other Lisbon Lions called him. Having spent some 20 years between the sticks with Queen's Park, Third Lanark, Newcastle and Hibs, Simpson joined Celtic at the age of 36 and won his first cap at the age of 37 (in the famous 3–2 defeat of England, newly crowned World Champions). Not the most flamboyant of characters in a team full of wags, he nonetheless got in on the act when, 30 yards out of his goal in the European Cup Final, with an Italian forward bearing down on him, he deftly cleared the danger with a cheeky back-heeler. After retiring he served as a member of the Pools Panel for more than 20 years and at the age of 60 was still coaching goalkeepers at a senior level.

TINY WHARTON

An unlikely role for a referee is that of hero, but the legendary Tiny Wharton of Clarkston, with his school master discipline, was a firm favourite of fans, if not the players. Here Celtic's Johnstone and Chalmers slink away after a typical Wharton wigging.

SHF 47

SHF 50

SHF 51

THE LISBON LIONS

Lisbon, 25 May 1967. The Italians, oiled and bronzed, looked like gods, their black and blue vertical-striped shirts emphasising their height in comparison with the squat-looking Celts in their green and white hoops. An unlovely bunch, Celtic had Ronnie Simpson with no teeth, a receding hairline and everybody else's false teeth in his bunnet, bow-legged Bertie Auld and freckled Jimmy Johnstone hustling Facchetti for a jersey swap at the end! The Italian's reacted with a mixture of bemusement and contempt as Auld led the team into the Celtic song, but 90 minutes later this ragbag of players - all from the west of Scotland, most from within 15 miles of Parkhead – had humbled the mighty Inter Milan 2 – 1 in what is perhaps the most outstanding achievement in Scottish sporting history. The exuberance and flamboyance of their play and the sheer magic of achievement – they were the first British team to win the European Cup – bestowed hero status on the club. Their attacking flair finally discredited the negative, defensive style promoted by Inter manager, Helenio Herrera. The pictures show McNeill and Murdoch with the cup at Parkhead and a team reunion for the 25th anniversary. Let the last word go to Bobby Lennox. "I felt quite confident. I had already put my teeth in Faither's bunnet because I thought we were going to win the European Cup and I wasn't going to have my picture taken without my teeth in." The reunion picture shows Jim Craig, Tommy Gemmell, Ronnie Simpson, Bobby Murdoch, Billy McNeill, John Clark, Jimmy Johnstone, Willie Wallace, Steve Chalmers, Bertie Auld and Bobby Lennox.

SHF 52

RANGERS IN BARCELONA

Rangers' greatest triumph was in 1972 when they added to Scotland's tally in Europe by beating Moscow Dynamo in Barcelona to win the European Cup Winners' Cup. En route to the final they took the scalps of notable European giants Bayern Munich, Torino and Sporting Lisbon. The crowd trouble which marred the end of the match resulted in a one year European ban, which sadly meant Rangers were unable to defend their title. The picture shows the squad: (top left to right) Gerry Neef, Dave Smith, Wille Mathieson, Derek Parlane, Colin Stein, John Greig, Derek Johnstone, Graeme Fyfe, (middle left to right) Alex MacDonald, Colin Jackson, Tommy McLean, Alfie Conn, Willie Johnstone, Ron McKinnon, Jim Denny, (front) Peter McCloy, Sandy Jardine, Andy Penman, Alex Miller.

SHF 42

DENIS McQUADE

A Partick Thistle legend who is proof that heroes exist at all levels in sport. Famous for his 'mazey runs' on the left wing, McQuade achieved cult status among the Firhill faithful. He scored in the famous 1971 League Cup Final victory over Celtic with a shot into a packed goalmouth. The ball found the net via a team-mate who was trying to duck!

DENIS LAW

With an unforgettable smile and an unforgettable, much-imitated accent, Denis Law was among the greats of the post-war Scots. A huge favourite of the fans, he was among the first British players to travel to the continent to escape the maximum wage limitations of the English league. After a year at Torino he was rescued by Matt Busby and came back to enormous success with Manchester United, becoming European Footballer of the Year in 1964. Now he is a popular radio and television commentator. Here he is being introduced to Glasgow's Lord Provost, John Mains, in 1972 by pocket battleship Billy Bremner, lynchpin of the famous Leeds United team of the 60s and 70s. Bremner was one of the many red headed terrier types that Scottish football seems to produce year after year.

SHF 53

SHF 54

WILLIE ORMOND

Ormond won a handful of caps in the 50s when he was part of Hibs' Famous Five forward line, though many felt he should have had more. He went on to a remarkably successful spell as manager of St Johnstone and then took over the Scotland side which he took to Germany in the 1974 World Cup. Although unbeaten, they did not qualify for the final stages.

WILLIE THORNTON

Regarded as one of the finest players to play for Rangers, Thornton made his debut in 1937 at the age of 16, and he remained close to the Ibrox club throughout his life. The war took seasons from his footballing life and on his return from the Army he settled in his famous partnership with Willie Waddell and Torry Gillick. A prolific scorer, he is best remembered for the spectacular goals which came from his head. He also enjoyed shoulder-charging jousts with goalkeepers – then a feature of the game – but he was a scrupulously clean player, invariably spoken of by opponents with affection and respect. He retired as a player in 1954 and had successful periods managing Dundee and Partick Thistle. Thornton returned to Rangers as assistant manager in 1968; his whole career was a refutation of the pernicious nonsense that in sport "nice guys don't win." He is seen here in the dugout with travelling rug at the ready, Harold Davis, a favourite right-half with the Ibrox legions in the early 60s, on his right.

SHF 55

SHF 56

SHF 43

ALFIE CONN

One of the first players to cross Scotland's barriers of hate, Alfie Conn played both for Rangers and Celtic, winning a Scottish Cup medal with both teams, Rangers in 1973 and Celtic in 1977. A skilful player, he is seen here in typical 70s style, long hair and big sideburns. Conn's father, also Alfie, played for Hearts along with Bauld and Wardhaugh. Conn junior was part of the Rangers team that won the European Cup Winners' Cup in Barcelona in 1972. He moved on to Spurs before signing for Celtic.

JOE HARPER

Joe Harper – the club's all-time top scorer – became a folk hero in Aberdeen during two spells at Pittodrie. He arrived from Morton in the 1960s' reign of manager Eddie Turnbull and returned in 1976 under manager Ally MacLeod in time for the League Cup win over Celtic. Between times he had gone to Everton for a record fee of £180,000, returning via Hibernian to regain his crown. The fans loved the bouncy, bubbly Joe, whose low centre of gravity assisted his amazing goal-scoring feats. In 1977, he overtook Harry Yorston's club record tally of 171 goals and extended it to 199. Curiously, he was not well favoured by manager Alex Ferguson and began to disappear from the Pittodrie scene just as Fergie launched the club towards European glory.

JOE JORDAN

The most famous toothless grin in football, Jordan was a firm favourite with Scotland supporters. Leading the line, he wore his courage openly; covered in mud, often bloodied, teeth missing and hair flying, here was someone you would want in your trench. He played for seven clubs (Morton, Leeds, Manchester United, AC Milan, Verona, Southampton and Bristol City) and has been successful as a manager and media pundit. Perhaps the most pragmatic factor in Jordan's favour as a sporting icon is that he barely played in Scotland, and so the entrenched loyalties of the Old Firm were never challenged. He enjoyed a 52-game Scottish career during which he scored goals at crucial times, not to mention earning a controversial penalty which allowed the crucial World Cup breakthrough against Wales at Anfield in 1977.

ALLY MacLEOD

World Cup team manager Ally Macleod receives the rapturous plaudits of a Hampden crowd . . . before a ball was kicked in the finals! This was the scene when more than 22,000 fans turned up for the team's send-off to the finals in Argentina in 1978. Cynics remarked that you would have thought they had won the Cup already. Sadly the hype back-fired and the disaster of Argentina to this day remains a traumatic memory for Scots. In his playing days Ally Macleod was a highly individualistic winger with Third Lanark, Blackburn and Hibs. Although something of an anti-hero as Scotland manager, he had several successful spells in management, particularly with Aberdeen.

SHF 57

SHF 58

ARCHIE GEMMILL

Archie Gemmill will always be remembered as the man who gave some dignity to the Scottish team amid the debacle in Argentina in the World Cup Finals. He scored a stunning individual goal against Holland, a goal so spectacular that it won an award as the best of the tournament, which at least gave the far-travelled Tartan Army something to sing about on the way home. Indeed that goal thrills fans to this day! A tenacious midfielder, he always gave 100 per cent, whether for Scotland or his clubs – Notts Forest, Derby, St Mirren and Preston.

SHF 59

DEREK JOHNSTONE

Big Derek Johnstone was a great favourite with Rangers and Scotland fans as a player. He has now built himself a career as a media pundit but this vintage shot shows him with Stewart Kennedy and Derek Parlane. Kipper ties, curly hair and big lapels were the order of the day as the Rangers squad prepared for a trip to Majorca.

SHF 60

SHF 61

JOCK WALLACE

Ironically his first association with Rangers was as the goalkeeper who played a major role in the biggest Scottish Cup upset of all time when Berwick Rangers beat the big Rangers 1–0 in 1967, a result that many who heard it on the radio assumed to be a mistake! A jungle fighter in Malaysia with the King's Own Scottish Borderers, he became a much-loved Rangers legend after he joined the Ibrox side in 1970 following a spell as assistant manager at Hearts. His record at Ibrox was phenomenal. Along with Willie Waddell he was part of the Cup Winners' Cup squad in Barcelona. Perhaps his major achievement was a double treble of League, Scottish Cup and League Cup in seasons 1976 and 1978. 'Big Jock', as the fans called him, was deeply mourned when he died in 1996.

DANNY McGRAIN
(opposite page)

A Celtic and Scotland fullback definitely up there with the greatest, McGrain was a brilliant and uncompromising tackler who is also remembered for his attacking play on the wing. He overcame both a bad skull fracture early in his career and diabetes to win 62 caps and many club honours. He has since become a symbol for aspiring sportsmen and women who suffer from diabetes. One of the few footballers to be hung in the National Portrait Gallery, McGrain also made a famous appearance on a television art appreciation programme in which he provided an eloquent interpretation of artist Phil Braham's 'The Chosen Way': "John (Dixie) Deans of Celtic missed a penalty kick against Inter Milan in the European Cup. Next morning there was a photo in the paper showing him alone at a bus stop – the lonely man in the big city. This print reminds me of that event." In this shot he is in an aerial tussle with Derek Johnstone.

SHF 62

ALAN ROUGH

The goalkeeper's lot can be lonely, especially on a snell, snow-flecked February day. A boy from Knightswood in Glasgow, who became one of Scotland's most capped keepers, Alan Rough's eccentric style found a natural home at Firhill where he became a great Partick Thistle favourite. 'Roughie' was a resilient, optimistic character who at the height of his career in 1981 won the Scottish Football Writers' Association Award as Player of the Year. After his playing days he went into junior football management and still plays an important role in the game.

CHARLIE NICHOLAS

Nicholas was one of the electrifying players whose skills packed stadiums for club matches but who never really made the mark in international football that his talents justified. His huge following at Celtic took it badly when he left to join Arsenal, although towards the end of his career 'Champagne Charlie' did return to Parkhead after a spell in Aberdeen. One of the most popular players of the 80s, he is seen here fending off Aberdeen's Willie Miller.

SHF 65

SHF 67

KENNY DALGLISH WITH TOMMY DOCHERTY AND ALEX FERGUSON

Scotland's most capped player with 102 appearances for his country, Kenny Dalglish had a razor-sharp footballing brain, tremendous strength and an outstanding ability to shield a ball while moving, a skill that made him almost impossible to mark out of a game. He went on successfully to manage Liverpool, Blackburn and Newcastle. He is seen here flanked by two other great managers, Tommy Docherty and Alex Ferguson. Docherty had a successful spell as manager of Manchester United and also briefly managed Scotland. The man about whom it was often said, not least by himself, that he had had more clubs than Jack Niklaus, is now a much sought-after after-dinner speaker. Ferguson made a name for himself as an opportunistic goal scorer for Rangers in the 60s. A straight-talking, no-nonsense Govan man, he is one of the most passionate managers in the game. After winning the European Cup Winners' Cup with Aberdeen he has achieved remarkable success with Manchester United, including League and Cup triumphs and the European Cup Winners' Cup again. (Inset: the famous Dalglish goal scoring grin).

SHF 64

ABERDEEN

Salute to heroes . . . Alex Ferguson and Archie Knox lead a charge by the Aberdeen bench celebrating their defeat of Real Madrid in Gothenburg in 1983 to win the European Cup Winners' Cup, a tremendous feat from the days when Scottish clubs regularly treated their fans to long runs in Europe. The club thrilled all Scotland as they scalped many of the greats during this successful period in Europe and John Hewitt's breathtaking winning header remains one of the great moments in Scotland's sporting history.

DUNDEE UNITED (opposite page)

Under the legendary Jim McLean, United won the League Championship for the first time in their history in 1983, and in true Roy of the Rovers style, clinched the title against arch rivals Dundee at Dens Park. Here McLean is saluted by some well-known Tannadice heroes, including Paul Sturrock, the young Richard Gough and Davie Dodds. This win kicked off a celebrated run in Europe, in which they reached the semi-final of the Champions' Cup in 1984 (gallantly losing away to Roma after a home win). In 1987 they convincingly beat Barcelona in the Nou Camp on the way to the final of the UEFA Cup, only to lose to Gothenburg. Their supporters, however, did not. Their sporting behaviour in staying on at Tannadice to applaud the winners, despite the pain of losing, astonished the Gothenburg team, and, in recognition, FIFA gave the club a financial award of £20,000. United used the money to build a family section at their ground. For a small club with little money, United provided all Scotland with some heroic European nights and, along with Aberdeen, they became part of the 'New Firm' which challenged the Rangers/Celtic domination of Scottish football.

McLEAN & STEWART
PAINTERS & DECORATORS

SHF 74

GRAEME SOUNESS

Graeme Souness was a vital part of the Liverpool team which won the European Cup in 1978, 1981 and 1984. He had started his career as an apprentice with Tottenham Hotspur but was transferred to Middlesbrough in 1972, helping his new club to win promotion in 1974. In June 1984 he signed for Sampdoria in Italy and then came back to Scotland in 1986 as player/manager of Rangers winning three League Championships there. He returned south to Liverpool (much to the annoyance of Rangers fans) but left after a spell as manager which did not produce the prolific successes demanded by the club's fans. He has also managed in Turkey and Italy. He is seen here with Rangers' high profile signings, Mo Johnston (centre) and Mark Hateley (right).

SHF 68

DAVIE COOPER

A rare breed in the modern game, Davie Cooper was never one for tackling or the physical side of the game. In fact, in the time-honoured football phrase, he could not tackle a fish supper. But this is no condemnation for a man who, according to his team-mate and manager John Greig, saw himself as an entertainer. His astounding natural skills on the left wing thrilled genuine supporters of every team. His ability to power, float or swerve the ball from set pieces was awesome. To Aberdeen keeper Jim Leighton's claim that he almost got to one scorching 22-yard free kick, Cooper humorously replied "Was that when it was coming back out of the net?" At the time of his death he was planning, in conjunction with his first and last club, Clydebank, to start the David Cooper Soccer School, which would have travelled the country preaching the gospel of skilful football to wide-eyed youngsters. Genius is always a joy to behold and Cooper was one of the few players who could force parents to take their children to matches. That in itself speaks volumes for the man, who died tragically in March 1995 at the age of 39 from a subarachnoid haemorrhage.

SHF 69

WILLIE MILLER AND GORDON STRACHAN

Willie Miller will remain unchallenged as the most important player in the history of Aberdeen FC. If manager Alex Ferguson was the architect of the Dons' Golden Era in the 80s it was Willie Miller who put it into practice as the captain. Breaking the monotonous mould of Rangers and Celtic, Miller then led his men against the might of Europe, bringing home the Cup Winners' Cup in 1983, beating the great Real Madrid in the Gothenburg final. It was a fairy tale come true. The strong, silent Miller, the Bridgeton boy who was originally a goalkeeper for Glasgow Schools, was signed by Aberdeen as a goal-scoring centre forward but found his niche as a defender, described by Alex Ferguson as "the best penalty-box player in the world". After two decades of legendary status the memory was slightly tarnished by a short and indifferent spell as the club's manager.

If Willie Miller was the defensive foundation of Aberdeen's Golden Era, Gordon Strachan was undoubtedly the creative genius, the red-headed buzz-bomb with the skill and confidence to beat players on his own and spread panic in the opposition. There may have been comparable ball-players in Pittodrie's history but none with the instinct to drive home the advantage. An Edinburgh lad, signed from Dundee by manager Billy NcNeill in 1977, Strachan arrived just months ahead of Alex Ferguson and became a key figure in shaping the route to European glory. That was never more evident than in the quarter-final of the European Cup Winners' Cup when his flash of inspiration brought Alex McLeish's equalising goal, leaving John Hewitt to notch the winner. It was the Pittodrie club's greatest occasion. Strachan preceded Ferguson to Manchester United in 1984 and went on to captain Leeds and then Coventry, a club which he later managed.

SHF 70

RICHARD GOUGH

Richard Gough is another candidate for the most successful captain in Rangers' history. Since his arrival at the club – which had turned him down as a youth – from Spurs in October 1987 for £1.5m, he lifted an amazing 13 trophies (six League Championships, three Scottish Cups and four League Cups) during his spell as skipper – one more than Ibrox legend Davie Meiklejohn in the 20s and 30s. Domestic glory was not echoed in European competition, but he enjoyed success with the national team, notably in Scotland's first European Championship finals in 1992. A fall-out with national coach Andy Roxburgh in 1993 after Scotand's 5–0 defeat by Portugal in a World Cup qualifier, and subsequent critical comments in his autobiography, ended his international career. Often bloodied and bruised, Richard Gough personifies the fighting spirit of Rangers. At a time when the habits and lifestyle of the modern professional footballer in Scotland were often called into question, Gough was one of the few who truly deserved the description model professional.

SHF 71

ALLY McCOIST

Idolised by fans, this perennial joker is also a firm favourite with the general public. Overcoming injuries, which included a broken leg, and a period out of favour under Graeme Souness, McCoist always managed to bounce back. The most prolific goal scorer in Ibrox history – with more than 300 goals – he holds the record of 11 Premier Division hat tricks. In December 1996 he scored his 265th league goal to set a new post-war record. Now in the twilight of his playing career he is never likely to be far from the public eye on retirement from the field.

SHF 73

SHF 72

TOMMY BURNS AND WALTER SMITH

The toughest game for any Rangers and Celtic manager is an Old Firm derby. The fans of both sides expect nothing less than complete supremacy. Here Tommy Burns and Walter Smith hide the inner tensions with a handshake and a private joke. Smith took Rangers to their ninth championship in a row in 1997. Tommy Burns, a great Celtic midfielder in the 80s, managed the club from 1994, leaving after season 1996–97 to join Kenny Dalglish at Newcastle.

PAUL McSTAY

Off the field Paul McStay was unassuming and not nearly as flamboyant as many of his contemporaries. On the field, however, he stamped his authority on the Celtic squad. A great club man, he also represented Scotland on many occasions. In the modern game McStay was one of that rare breed which spends its entire career with one club. He was a great servant for Celtic, though sadly injury ended his career.

THE NOBLE ART

TANCY LEE

Perhaps it has something to do with a history of poverty and under-nutrition but Scotland has held a stranglehold on the British flyweight championship (for 8 stone fighters) ever since Paisley-born Tancy Lee became the first Scot to win it way back in 1914. This shot shows him with the famous Italian heavyweight giant Primo Carnera at a promotion in the Marine Gardens Ballroom, Edinburgh.

TOMMY MILLIGAN

This picture of Milligan (left) with a sparring partner training for a fight in London captures the flavour of boxing in the 20s when working class men fought their way to wealth. Milligan, who had a huge following on the south side of Glasgow, was another Scot who narrowly failed to win a world title, losing to the great Mickey 'Toy Bulldog' Walker in 1927.

JOHNNY HILL

From Strathmiglo in Fife, Johnny Hill was the first Scot to be named as world champion contender. He won the European Flyweight title in 1929, a feat not equalled until Pat Clinton lifted the title in 1990. Sadly he died shortly after taking ill during preparations for a fight with the American flyweight Frankie Genaro in the late 1920s.

ELKY CLARK

A wonderful 1920s shot of Elky Clark with his trainer Puggy Morgan, an early exponent of the braces over the pullover! Elky, another of Scotland's tiny terrors, had his biggest moment in New York's Madison Square Garden in 1927 when he narrowly failed to wrest the world flyweight title from Fidel LaBarba. His ring career over, Elky turned to journalism as a boxing writer.

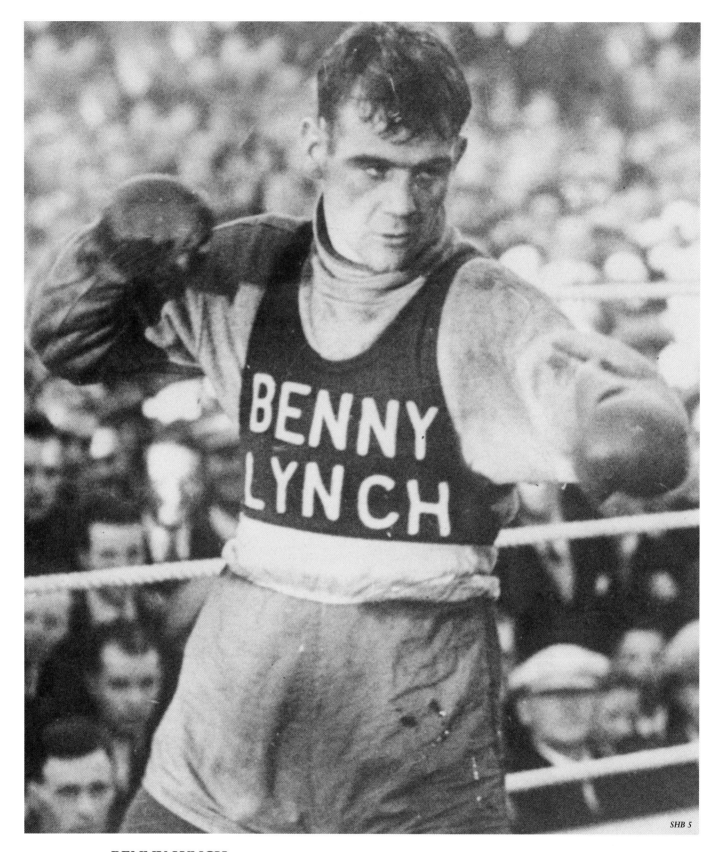

SHB 5

BENNY LYNCH

The first Scot to win a world title when he beat Jackie Brown in 1935. Benny was such a naturally talented boxer than when he lifted the world title he had only been a pro for four years. He was a flyweight with a devastating punch. A flawed hero, his career went into a rapid decline and he died at 33, a tragic figure beaten by drink. His memory has lived on in plays and books and rumours of a film of his life surface from time to time.

JACKIE PATERSON

At the height of his boxing career the legendary scrapper from Springfield, Ayrshire, held five major titles and in boxing circles was thought to be one of the greatest fighters of his time. In a famous fight he knocked out English challenger Peter Kane in just 61 seconds. Paterson was murdered in Johannesburg in 1966 at the age of 46. In this picture he is seen with Benny Lynch, standing at the far right in a crumpled suit, perhaps not looking his best.

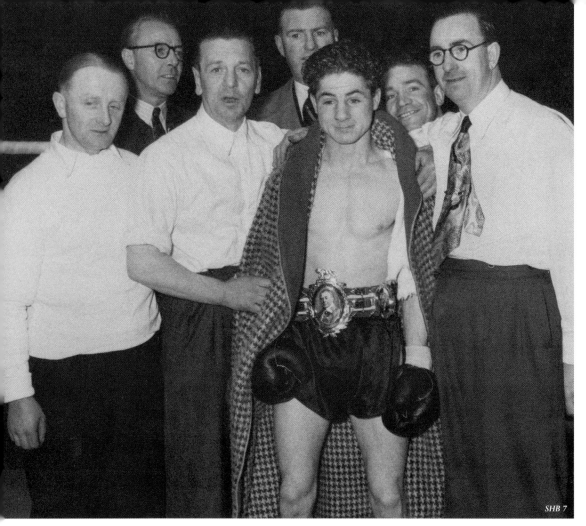

SHB 7

PETER KEENAN

Known as 'PK' to fight fans, Peter Keenan had a huge Glasgow following and often fought in the open air at football stadiums. A pawky character, he was a major figure in city life in and out of the ring. Here he looks well-satisfied after a night's boxing, his Lonsdale Belt to the fore. On his left is Tommy Gilmour, himself a legendary Glasgow character. In 1952 Peter Keenan narrowly missed out winning the World Championship, being beaten on points by Vic Toweel in South Africa.

SHB 8

DICK McTAGGART

Said by some to be the greatest amateur boxer Britain has produced, Dick McTaggart refused all offers to turn pro. He didn't pack a huge punch but had a tremendous ability to jab, scoring points off rougher opponents and staying out of trouble. He won Olympic gold (1956) and bronze (1960) medals and fought both as a lightweight and a light welterweight. A superb stylist and a delight to watch, he was given an award as the outstanding stylist of the Melbourne Olympics in 1956. He went on to coach the Scottish team for the Commonwealth Games.

'COWBOY' JOHN McCORMACK

'Cowboy' John McCormack was a contemporary of Chick Calderwood. McCormack won the British and European middleweight titles. From Glasgow's Maryhill – he was proud to be a 'Butney' boy – he had memorable battles with England's Terry Downes winning one on a disqualification but losing the rematch.

CHICK CALDERWOOD

From Craigneuk in Lanarkshire, Chick Calderwood, who was managed by his father, Tommy, became the British and Commonwealth light heavyweight champion. One curious event in this marvellous boxer's career was that he fought Henry Cooper's twin brother in the Kelvin Hall in 1961. He died in a car crash in 1966.

SHB 9

SHB 10

SHB 11

WALTER McGOWAN

McGowan, from Burnbank, Lanarkshire, was from a famous boxing family. Both his father, who was a major influence on his career and had himself fought under the name Joe Gans, and his brothers often acted as seconds. Here Walter is seen with two other boxing legends, Peter Keenan on his right, and a boyish Cassius Clay, later Mohammed Ali, during the heavyweight champ's visit to Glasgow in 1965. A flyweight, McGowan lost only two of his 124 amateur contests – a remarkable record. Then he went on to win the WBC world title in 1966, beating Salvatore Burruni of Italy on points. In 40 professional contests, he won 32, 14 by knockout, and drew once. Later in his career cuts caused him some bother and after leaving the ring he became a popular publican.

SHB 12

JIM WATT AND KEN BUCHANAN

Scotland produced two of the world's finest lightweights when the careers of Ken Buchanan and Jim Watt overlapped. Here they are after the British title fight in 1973 won by Buchanan (right). Watt regained the British title in 1977 and went on to win the WBC title against Alfredo Pitalua of Colombia in the Kelvin Hall, Glasgow. He had a spectacular run of four successful defences of his title – winning three inside the distance – but was finally beaten by Alexis Arguello of Nicaragua in 1981. A brilliant public speaker, Watt made a new career for himself as a television boxing commentator. Ken Buchanan, for his part, won the British recognised version of the world lightweight title by beating Ismael Laguna.

SHB 14

GARY JACOBS

Glasgow south-sider Gary Jacobs has had something of a roller-coaster career in which he won Scottish, British, Commonwealth and European titles at welterweight after becoming a professional in 1987. He moved from welterweight to middleweight but unfortunately failed to take the title at this level. At times underestimated during his career, he nonetheless became a big favourite with the home fans.

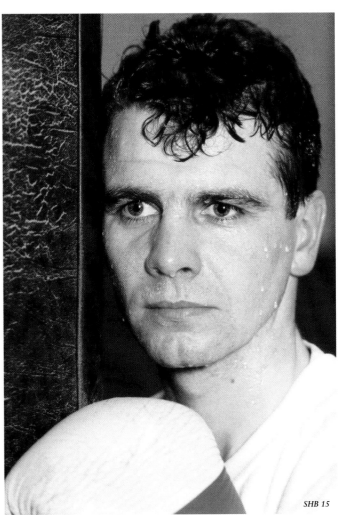

SHB 15

PAT CLINTON

Pat Clinton enjoyed a glittering career in which he won Scottish, British, European and WBO world featherweight titles. The Croy hero went on to play football in charity games for Dukla Pumpherston which boasts the like of Danny McGrain, Alex MacDonald and Tommy McLean. Fittingly for someone of his weight, he also harboured ambitions to be a jockey.

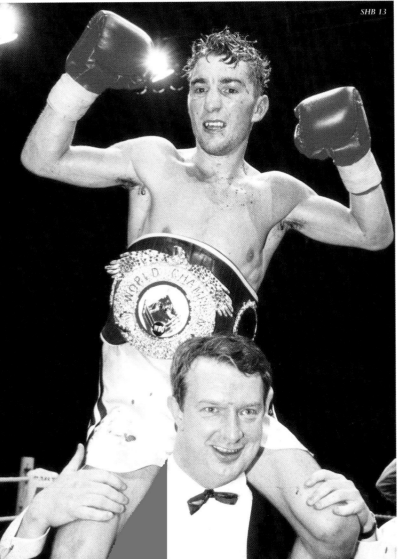

SHB 13

PAUL WEIR

A mighty atom in the ring, Irvine's Paul Weir won world titles at both straw-weight and light flyweight. Here he is celebrating on the shoulders of boxing promotor Tommy Gilmour, who followed his father, also called Tommy, to become a dominant figure on the Glasgow fight scene.

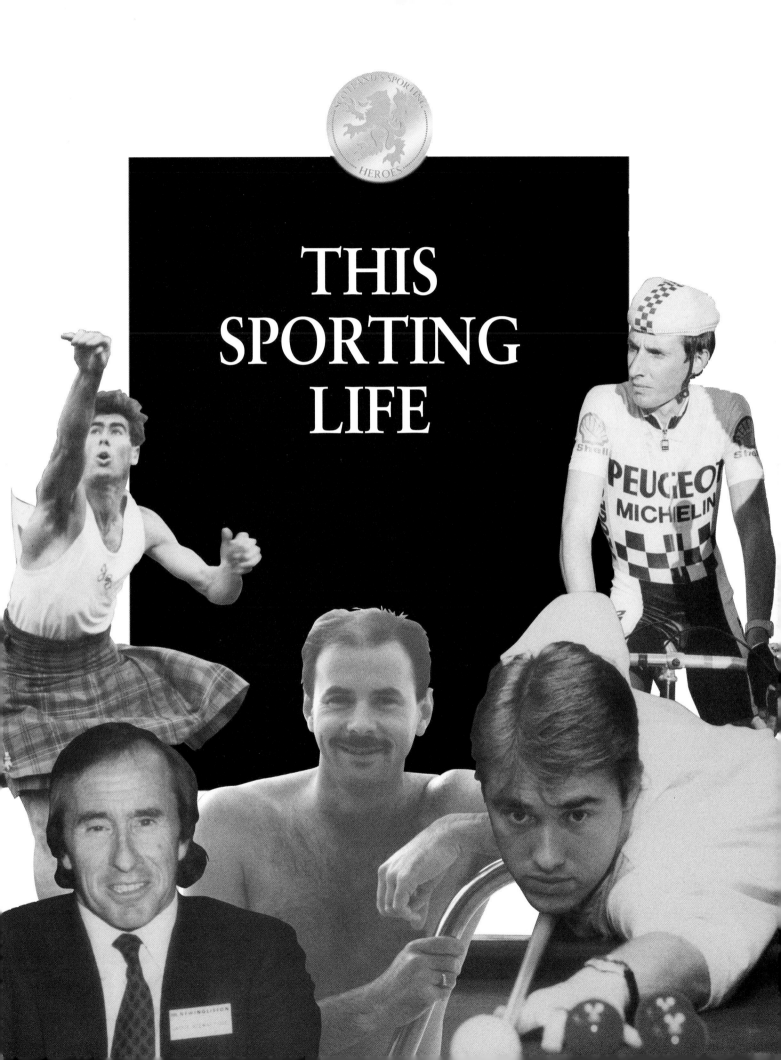

THIS
SPORTING
LIFE

SHM 1

RICHARD CORSIE

An Edinburgh postman, Corsie has won a sackload of trophies since becoming Scottish Junior Bowls Champion in 1983: six world titles, a Commonwealth gold medal and two Mazda Jack High wins. He is equally at home on indoor carpet or bumpy, bare greens.

SHM 2

JOCKY WILSON

Darts was a sport that moved from the pub to the television and Jocky Wilson was one of the first exponents of the game to become a household name. Despite a distinctly unathletic appearance, many darts players were revered as true sporting heroes. Fifer Jocky made it to the very top as world champion. He is seen here in 1995 with Eric Bristow (right), known as the 'Crafty Cockney' in the smoke-filled world of flying arrows.

SHM 3

STEPHEN HENDRY

Taking over the mantle of the world's greatest snooker player from Steve Davis, the first of Hendry's many world titles came in 1990 when he was just 21. A great favourite of television snooker fans, he was said to be the son every mother wanted – presentable, mannerly and earning prodigious sums of money. He started playing at the age of 12 and was soon breaking records. At 15 he was the youngest Scottish amateur champion and he went on to become the youngest winner of a ranking tournament.

WINNIE WOOLDRIDGE (SHAW)

Scotland can boast few tennis players of international stature. Daughter of Winnie Mason Shaw – who herself was a tennis champion in the 1930s – Winnie Wooldridge, better known as Winnie Shaw in her day, is Scotland's most successful woman tennis player. At her peak she was ranked third in Britain and reached the quarter-finals of the singles and semi-finals of the ladies' doubles at Wimbledon. Not content with that she also played golf at international level. Tragically she died of a brain haemorrhage in 1992 at the age of 45.

FRANCES McLENNAN

Another woman who acquitted herself well on the tennis court, Frances McLennan was still playing in over-40s events in 1991. At one time she was married to British tennis star Roger Taylor.

SHM 5

SHM 9

NANCY RIACH

Nancy Riach of Motherwell was once described as the finest swimmer in the British Empire. Tragically she died at the age of 20 in 1947 while representing Great Britain in the European Championships in Monte Carlo, a victim of polio. A wonder girl in all swim strokes, she held 28 British and Scottish records in 1945.

HELEN ORR GORDON

Helen Orr Gordon (she became known as 'Eleanor' for short!) was the talented daughter of the Hamilton baths manager and in 1952 won a bronze medal in the 200m breaststroke event in the Helsinki Olympics. From 1947 until 1957 Eleanor was Scottish 200m breaststroke champion. In 1950 she received the Nancy Riach memorial medal for her services to swimming.

BOBBY McGREGOR

Bobby McGregor MBE is now working as an architect in Glasgow. He was one of Britain's few world class swimmers in 1964 when he took silver in the 100m freestyle in the Olympic games. The Falkirk Otters swimmer was six times British Sprint Champion and was a silver medalist in the 1962 and 1966 Commonwealth Games. He was a World Student Games medalist in 1966. Here he is coaching at Whiteinch Baths, where many Glasgow west-enders first tasted chlorine!

CATHY GIBSON

Cathy Gibson was a member of the fabulous Motherwell Swim Club which dominated not only Scottish but British swimming in the 40s and 50s. She followed in the trail of tragic Nancy Riach and made the 1948 Olympics in London, where she won a bronze medal in the 400m freestyle. The Motherwell club had seven of its members in those Olympics competing in swimming and water polo. The club had a renowned 'Water Circus' which toured Britain, with people flocking to attend their performances to watch their swimming skills and routines.

SHM 8

DAVID WILKIE

David Wilkie earned the title of Golden Boy of Swimming for his amazing achievements in 1976 when he became Olympic Champion in the 200m breast-stroke, having come second in the same event four years earlier. Wilkie was born in Ceylon (now Sri Lanka) but came to Scotland with his family to swim for the Warrender Club in Edinburgh. However, his world class skills were honed at Miami University: he set a world record in the 200m breaststroke in 1973 and became world champion the same year. Two years later he was double world champion at the 100m and 200m. He broke his own world record in the 200m breaststroke in 1976 – his golden year.

SHM 13

JIMMIE GUTHRIE

Known as the 'Flying Scotsman', Jimmie Guthrie was Norton's top professional in the mid 30s and the number one racing motor cyclist of this era. A modest, much loved man, he died in the 1937 German Grand Prix when he crashed mysteriously while in the lead and almost in sight of the winning flag. An Isle of Man TT legend, Jimmie is remembered by a roadside memorial on the climb out of Ramsay.

SHM 14

RON FLOCKHART AND NINIAN SANDERSON

Flockhart started out in motor cycle racing but made his name in cars driving in the old Formula Libre and in Formula One in a BRM. He won Le Mans in 1956 in a Jaguar, driving with Ninian Sanderson (right), a victory he repeated the next year with Ivor Bueb as his co-driver. He was killed in a plane crash practising for a London to Sydney record attempt.

SHM 15

JIM CLARK

Ironically the man who is, with Jackie Stewart, a contender for the title of the greatest motorsport Scot, died in an unimportant race at Hockenheim in 1968 at the tragically young age of 32. Jim Clark was an extremely versatile driver who was a winner at Indianapolis and in sports cars as well in the Formula One Lotus which brought him his greatest successes. Three times world Formula One champion, Clark was a true hero, combining great skill and courage with modesty. He also had a sense of humour and as a young man enjoyed driving an unimposing looking Lotus Cortina up the A1, picking off drivers of apparently faster, flashier cars, leaving them wondering what on earth was going on.

SHM 16

JIM CLARK
ORLD CHAMPION
3-INDIANAPOLIS-196

73

SHM 17

JACKIE STEWART

Three times world champion in Formula One (1969, 1971 and 1973), and winner of 27 Grand Prix races, Jackie Stewart now has his own Grand Prix team. From a family involved in the car world and based in Dumbarton, he also starred in the Indianapolis 500. A crack clay pigeon shooter, his eyesight was legendary: he could spot faces in the crowd while travelling at three figure speeds. During his career he fought to introduce many of the safety features taken for granted in modern Grand Prix racing. Courteous, dapper and dedicated, he had a long association with Ford after retiring at the very top of his profession, something many sportsmen do not have the good sense to do.

SHM 18

LOUISE AITKEN-WALKER

Louise Aitken-Walker is another in a long line of motor sport stars from the Scottish Borders. During the 80s she was the first woman to win a British national-status rally, she took the ladies' award three times on the RAC Rally and once on the Monte Carlo, twice won her class in the British Open Rally Championship, and managed a full season's racing in touring cars. All this culminated in her European Ladies Rally Championship victory with Vauxhall in 1989. In 1991 she was top British driver on the RAC Rally, and started 1992 by being awarded the MBE.

DAVID COULTHARD

Coulthard developed an early taste for success at the age of 11 as Scottish Junior Kart Champion. By 1989 he was competing in the Brands Hatch Formula Ford Festival, finishing third, the highest ever placing for a junior. He started the 1994 season as test driver for Williams but, on the death of Ayrton Senna, was given a shot at Grand Prix, competing in eight races and amassing 14 World Championship points to finish eighth. He continues to keep Scottish hopes alive as a Formula One driver for McLaren.

SHM 19

SHM 20

SHM 21

RUBSTIC

A hero on four legs. Rubstic is the only Scottish trained winner in the history of the Grand National. He was 26 when he died in his stable in Ladykirk, between Berwick and Coldstream, where he had lived under the care of former trainer, John Leadbetter. Here Rubstic enjoys the adulation of his home fans in 1979 after he had carried Maurice Barnes to a length-and-a-half triumph over Zongalero in the National. Rubstic was owned throughout his career by former international rugby player, John Douglas.

WILLIE CARSON

Not too many Scots make it to the top in horse racing. Willie Carson, from Stirling, was the first Scot to be Champion Jockey, winning five times from 1972. His consistently cheery demeanour made him something of a television star in the BBC's *Question of Sport*. Like all jockeys, the punters lauded his victories but they were, as always, unforgiving over defeats. Later in his career he fought back from serious injury, winning the admiration not only of racing people but of the public at large.

SANDY BARCLAY

Sandy Barclay had a great start to his racing career which turned out to be briefer than that enjoyed by most jockeys. Apprenticed to Harry Whiteman at Ayr, his first winner came in May 1965 and by the next year he was the Champion Apprentice. In 1967, when George Moore returned to Australia, Sandy took over as number one jockey for Noel Murless. He won three classics – The Thousand Guineas on Caergwrle, The King George VI and Queen Elizabeth Stakes on Royal Palace and the 1970 Oaks on Lupe.

GEORGE BOYD

At the height of his career George Boyd was Scotland's biggest and most successful flat race trainer. When he retired in 1969 he had saddled 700 winners. Rockaven was his only classic success, in winning the Two Thousand Guineas at an official starting price of 66–1, although, in fact, the Tote paid 108–1.

NIGEL ANGUS

Nigel Angus, former master of Cree Lodge racing stables in Ayr who had started in racing as an assistant to Harry Whiteman, knew more than most about winning the Ayr Gold Cup. In 1975 it was Angus who took the great Roman Warrior to the winner's enclosure. He sent animals to Goodwood, Ascot, Cheltenham and Newcastle, churning out winners for delighted owners. After racing he devoted much of his attention to his family's substantial farming interest.

SHM 25

FREUCHIE

Good Lords we done it! The boys from Freuchie are led by skipper David Christie off the hallowed turf at Lords after winning the National Village Cricket Championship. The year was 1985 and the Scots took the trophy for the first time at the expense of Rowledge from Surrey. Success came in the last over when, with the scores tied at 134 but with two wickets in hand, Freuchie held out for a fantastic victory. Scottish Television paid for an extra night in London after the victory to prepare a documentary on Freuchie at Lords, making them TV stars into the bargain.

COLIN McRAE AND OTHERS

This group of Scots live life in the fast lane. Gathered together for a charity go-karting night are, (top, left to right) Niall McKenzie, motor cycle Grand Prix star, Donnie McLeod, a Scottish kart champion, Richard Devine, the Scottish MX Champion, and Ian Simpson, British Superbike Champion, along with (front) the two McRae brothers, Colin and Alistair, with Ford driver Nigel Feeney in the car. The McRae family, from father Jimmy onwards, have made a tremendous mark in rallying. Colin was the youngest winner of the World Rally Championship in 1995 while father Jimmy was five times British Champion.

ROBERT MILLAR

Few Scots have made such a mark in cycling as Robert Millar, seen here during a Kellog's city centre race in Glasgow, his home city. He shot to prominence in the Tour de France in the 1980s when he won several stages and took the coveted King of the Mountains jersey, the first Briton to do so. His best finish in cycling's greatest event was fourth, while Millar also had considerable success in various Kellog's Tour of Britain races. He settled in France towards the end of his professional career and is now Britain's National Road Coach.

SHM 26

BILL ANDERSON

Anderson was star of that most Scottish of institutions, the Highland Games. Had he kicked a ball rather than thrown a hammer he might have become more of a hero outwith his own parish. He made his debut at 15 in 1959, winning nine pounds and ten shillings, which he reckons he spent that night – what a night! He was Scottish champion 15 times and travelled the world to pursue and promote his sport.

SHM 27

JAY SCOTT

Jay Scott, who died in 1997, dominated the Highland Games scene in the late 50s and early 60s until a tractor accident ended his athletics career. As a boy, he lived on Inchmurrin on Loch Lomond and with his brother, Tom, helped rescue many a stricken tourist from the Loch. He was a record-holding high jumper as well as being a winner at most of the Highland Games disciplines. He married actress Fay Lenore who was a star in the old Glasgow Alhambra's famous Five Past Eight shows.

STROKES
OF
GENIUS

JAMES BRAID

Golf has moved a long way from the days when you could spot a bowler hat in the gallery and the star wore a collar and tie on the tee. Here is the legendary James Braid of Waltonheath in action in 1919. Braid was the last home-born Scot to win The Open title back in 1910. When his playing career was over he became an early exponent of the player-turned-golf-course-architect, with input into many famous courses throughout the world, including Gleneagles.

SHG 1

TOMMY ARMOUR

The famous 'Silver Scot' who won The Open in 1931, though it has to be said that at the time of his win Armour was one of a small army of Scots professionals who had sailed to the New World and by this time he was, in fact, an American citizen. Armour wrote highly successful teaching manuals that had huge sales on both sides of the Atlantic. One of his bestremembered comments was "As ye waggle so shall ye swing".

SHG 2

EDDIE HAMILTON AND SAM McKINLAY

Two of the most distinguished of the pre-war amateurs. Sam McKinlay of Western Gailes polishes up his putting prior to a British Amateur Championship at Hoylake watched by Eddie Hamilton (Ralston and Western Gailes) who also had an amateur career at the highest level before becoming a much - respected newspaper journalist. Sam McKinlay was also a distinguished Editor of the *Evening Times*. Both still found time to carve great golfing careers.

SHG 3

DR FRANK DEIGHTON

A star player much admired for his swing, Frank Deighton dominated Scottish amateur golf for a long period. Famed for his dedication to practice, his home courses were Hilton Park and Western Gailes and as well as winning regularly on the domestic amateur circuit, he played in the Walker Cup.

SHG 4

HECTOR THOMSON

Thomson is pictured here playing at Douglas Park in the 1950s when a collar and tie was still the dress code on the golf course although by now it appears you were allowed to slacken off the collar. Hector was one of the few top Scottish amateurs who switched early in his career to join the professional ranks where he had respectable success. He taught golf for a spell in Egypt.

HAMMY McINALLY

The original caption on this typical action shot of McInally respectfully refers to him as Mr Hamilton McInally. Hammy, whose huge legion of fans were the Ayrshire equivalent of Arnie's army, had the remarkable distinction of having two golfing handicaps. He played off 1 right-handed and played off 3 left-handed and in club competitions he had to nominate which way he would play. From Barton Holme by Irvine, he won the Scottish Amateur three times in a career disrupted by the war.

SHG 5

SHG 6

MAJOR DAVID BLAIR

Major David Blair from Nairn was known as an elegant swinger and an elegant dresser with a military bearing on and off the course. Among his victories was the Scottish Amateur in 1953, while in 1950 at the Troon Open he won the Amateur Medal, a feat repeated by another prominent Scottish amateur, Barclay Howard, again at Troon in 1997. Blair played in two Walker Cups in 1955 and 1961.

ERIC BROWN

A vintage swing from Eric Brown practising at Duddingston in 1969. A former railway fireman from Bathgate and a battler on the course, he was often at odds with golf's establishment but he was a huge favourite of the cloth-capped golfing galleries of the day. His best Open finish was third in 1957 and he made four Ryder Cup appearances from 1953 to 1959 winning all of his four singles matches – a mark of what a great competitor he was (his foursome record was less successful).

HARRY BANNERMAN

The Cruden Bay professional, Bannerman had the skills to take him to a top international career but his progress was blighted with a fight against back injury. Nonetheless he inspired many Scots in the 1960s and was noted for his frequent comments about his own game – he described his iron shots as "one majestic blow after another".

SHG 9

R. D. B. M. SHADE

Two of the greatest names in Scottish golf photographed during the Scottish Amateur at Carnoustie in 1967. A boyish Bernard Gallacher (left) was just beginning his career but Ronnie Shade was nearing the end of an astonishing series of five successful wins in the Amateur, which included an amazing record of 44 match-play victories in a row. His initials R. D. B. M. stood for Ronald David Bell Mitchell but became an acronym for 'Right Down the Bloody Middle' which was remarkably apt considering his solid, consistent style of play. The son of a pro, John Shade, who was at Duddingston for many years, Ronnie later turned pro himself with some success. He died at the early age of 47.

SHG 10

DAVID HUISH

Born and brought up in the golfing town of Gullane, David Huish never played as an amateur and never had a handicap. He left school at 17 and entered the Scottish Assistant's Championship in 1962. In 1975 he led the Open Championship at Carnoustie at the half-way mark but finished 30th. He played in the Great Britain and Ireland team for club pros nine times and has the distinction of having won more points for his team against the Americans than any other pro.

SHG 12

CHARLIE GREEN

A fine shot of Charlie Green driving at Gullane during the home internationals in the late 1960s. His partner Gordon Cosh is immediately to the left of Green. Charlie had a long and distinguished career at club and international level and at one stage was almost unbeatable on the West of Scotland amateur circuit.

JACK CANNON AND JIMMY WALKER

Seen here with the magnificent *Evening Times* Foursomes Shield won at Bogside in 1962, Jack Cannon (left) is famous as the oldest Scottish amateur champion, winning aged 54. Jimmy Walker is wearing his Walker Cup blazer with pride. Oddly, Cannon, Walker and another Ayrshire legend, Hammy McInally, all came from a little village near Irvine Ravenspark golf club. Must have been something in the air!

SHG 11

SHG 13

BERNARD GALLACHER

The highlight of Bernard Gallacher's distinguished career was his involvement with Ryder Cup. Perhaps the peak of his career was to be appointed non-playing Ryder Cup Captain in 1991, 1993 and 1995 when, famously, he won on American soil. Bernard is shown here at a press call with the great Tom Watson, captain of the victorious 1993 American team. Previously he had played in the Cup with a record of 13 wins, 13 losses and five halves. Like the formidable Eric Brown he came from Bathgate, and had a distinguished career as an amateur before turning pro and becoming the youngest ever Ryder Cup player at 20. He had 13 European Tour victories from 1964 to 1984.

SHG 17

SANDY LYLE

The last Scot to win The Open at Royal St Georges in 1985, Lyle was actually born in England and played for the land of his birth as an amateur, but Sandy's Scottish roots are as solid as his Scottish mansion. He also won the US Masters in 1988, sealing a thrilling victory with one of the most famous and best-remembered bunker shots in the history of golf. His one iron off the tee left him way short of the green in a huge bunker. Rather than splash out Lyle put a seven iron to 10ft and sank the putt. Never was a green jacket won in more spectacular fashion. He has also played in the Ryder Cup and achieved five US Tour victories.

BELLE ROBERTSON

From Southend, Argyll, Belle Robertson ended a spectacular sequence of second places in the British Ladies Amateur by winning in 1981 – becoming the oldest champion at 45. A true legend in Scotland's ladies golf, she appeared in the Curtis Cup no fewer than seven times. Confirming the affection the Scottish golfing public felt for her was the fact that she was voted Scotland's Sportswoman of the Year four times.

SHG 14

SHG 15

JOHN AND CATHY PANTON

One of the legends of Scottish golf watches his daughter Cathy, no doubt ready to give her a few tips. John Panton won the Scottish Professional Championship six times in the 1940s and 50s and played in the Ryder Cup. Cathy was a winner on the Ladies Pro Tour. He also gave his name to a popular golf club soft drink – ask for a 'John Panton' and up comes a chilled ginger beer and lime.

SHG 18

SHG 19

COLIN MONTGOMERIE

Perhaps the finest golfer never to win a major – so far – Montgomerie was highly fancied for a fairytale win in the Open at Troon in 1997, the course where he learned to play, but it was not to be. However, Colin has represented Scotland at the highest level in tournaments worldwide and features strongly at the top of the world rankings. Often controversial, his will to win has on occasion worked against him.

SAM TORRANCE

The Largs man who retained the common touch, Torrance could lay claim to the title of Scotland's favourite golfer. That, of course, would be in addition to the barrow-load of other titles he has won at European and world level. A regular in the European Ryder Cup team since 1981, his triumphant victory salute after his glorious winning putt at the Belfry in 1985 was one of sport's great moments. He is seen here with his trademark long-handled putter.

CHARIOTS
OF
FIRE

WYNDHAM HALSWELLE

Wyndham Halswelle lined up in the Olympic 400 metres final in London in 1908 against three Americans, one of whom, John Carpenter, ran him wide and was disqualifed – they did not run in lanes in those days. The two other Americans refused to compete in the re-run, and Halswelle became the only walk-over Olympic champion. He was killed by a sniper in World War I but to this day Scottish junior boys compete for a 400 metres trophy in his memory.

SHA 1

ERIC LIDDELL
(opposite page)

The film *Chariots of Fire* took the Eric Liddell story to a new audience but his fame was secure in Scottish folklore long before the film – Liddell's gold in the 400 metres in the 1924 Olympics saw to that. At the Scottish Championships he won the 100 and the 220 yards for five successive years and his 100 yards personal best of 9.7 seconds lasted as a British record for 35 years. Born in China in 1902, he returned to join his father as a missionary in 1925 and died there in 1945 while interned in a Japanese concentration camp. Here he is seen crossing the tape at Ibrox Park.

DUNKIE WRIGHT

An exceptional marathon runner who won a gold medal at the inaugural Empire Games in Canada and dominated distance running in Scotland in the early 1930s, Dunkie Wright, a forceful administrator, became an outstanding official of the Scottish Amateur Athletics Association over a number of years, always working with the interests of athletes of all ages in mind. Here he is seen with Ernest Harper of England and an admiring crowd. No Nike logos or vast advertising in those days!

SHA 3

SHA 2

SHA 4

JOE McGHEE

Joe McGhee of Shettleston Harriers was another Scottish marathon marvel. Here in June 1955 he receives a laurel wreath from Mrs Gough, daughter of the then President of the SAAA, for yet another victory. Joe won Empire Games gold in 1954, beating Jim Peters, his arch rival, the great English distance man.

JIM ALDER

Scotland's marathon hero, Jim Alder won gold in the 1966 Commonwealth Games in Jamaica, and silver in Edinburgh four years later, feats achieved on training done after ten-hour shifts as a bricklayer. There were no huge financial rewards in Alder's era, and he was famously involved in a controversy over the payment of expenses in the zealously amateur days of the late 1970s. Alder, still laying bricks after the failure of his Morpeth sports shop, makes no secret of wishing that current rewards had been available in his day.

SHA 6

SHA 7

SHA 19

SHA 5

GRAHAM EVERETT (left)

Eight-time Scottish mile champion, Everett went on to coach Carol Sharp, wife of sprinter Cameron. His was a real sporting family. Daughter Andrea ran in the Commonwealth Games 10,000 metres, son Craig is a profesional golfer and his wife Hilda was a Commonweath Games team manager.

MENZIES CAMPBELL (right)

Better known these days as the debonair Liberal Democrat MP for North-East Fife, in his youth Ming Campbell was a champion sprinter who represented Britain at the 1964 Tokyo Olympics and held the British 100 metres record from 1967 to 1974. Along with contemporary Les Piggott he was also well known on the black cinder track at the Cowal Highland Games. He is seen here combining academic garb with his athletic skills.

CRAWFORD FAIRBROTHER

Scotland has a habit of finding remarkable double acts and for a time high jumping was the big attraction at sports meetings. Here Crawford Fairbrother jumps 6ft 5in in the Scottish AAA Championships at New Meadowbank in Edinburgh in the 1960s. A weatherman, Fairbrother was often said by the hacks of the day to be jumping into the clouds. The other outstanding high jumper of that time was Alan Paterson, whose talent showed earlier than most – he won a European medal a month after his 17th birthday.

MIKE HILDREY

Scots are great people for awarding sportsmen nicknames. Here is Mike Hildrey, known in his heyday as the 'Balfron Bullet', winning a heat in the 120 yards invitation at the famous Rangers Sports in 1961. This annual event at Ibrox was extremely popular, marking the end of the athletics season and the start of the football campaign. Mike Hildrey made his mark in the old European and Empire Games and on retiring from the track became one of Scotland's foremost investigative journalists with the *Evening Times*.

GEORGE McNEILL

A remarkable picture from the files shows George McNeill, the greatest professional runner Scotland ever produced and at one time said to be the world's fastest sprinter, in action against a race horse in Meadowbank in 1971. He would almost certainly have won Olympic gold had he been an amateur. He did on one occasion try for reinstatement but he had been a professional footballer with Hibs and the rule book allowed no way back. How different it would be now in these days of cash for titles. The ultimate McNeill irony is that towards the end of his career as a professional he was earning less than many 'amateurs'.

LACHIE STEWART, IAN STEWART AND IAN McCAFFERTY

In 1970, Edinburgh hosted a quite magnificent Commonwealth Games where such as Lachie Stewart, Ian McCafferty, Ian Stewart, and Rosemary Stirling thrilled the nation and became role models for others. Lachie, seen here proudly showing off his medal, won the 10,000 metres in swaggering style and continues to run today.

On a rain-soaked track in the days before high tech footwear, Ian Stewart (no 316 below) stormed home to take gold in the 5000 metres with Ian McCafferty close behind to land silver. Also a European champion, he is seen here with Rosemary Stirling who took the gold in the 800 metres. It is a commentary on the state of the sport in Scotland that the Scottish records by McCafferty, Lachie Stewart, Jim Alder and Stirling remained unbeaten in 1997.

SHA 12

FRANK CLEMENT

Frank Clement was a top-rated middle-distance athlete during the 1970s when he competed in the Olympics and the Commonwealth Games for Scotland. The mile and 1500-metre record breaker was also the first British runner to win the Europa Cup.

LESLIE PIGGOTT AND DAVID JENKINS

Olympic sprinter Les Piggott of Garscube Harriers, often known as Lester after his jockey namesake, was a popular figure on the Scottish circuit of the 1960s. He won a record number of Glasgow sprints and defied modern convention by smoking throughout his athletics career. On his left is David Jenkins who became European 400 metres champion in 1977 and took relay silver in the 1972 Olympics. He was later disgraced after becoming involved in a steroids scandal in the USA.

SHA 11

SHA 14

GRAHAM WILLIAMSON

Williamson was in the unfortunate position of being a world class miler when in this class there was a surfeit of supermen, such as Sebastian Coe and Steve Ovett. He is seen here at a Highland Games meeting at Meadowbank in 1978 just ahead of Frank Clement at the tape.

SHA 13

ALLAN WELLS

When the Americans boycotted the 1980 Olympics in Moscow Allan Wells, at 28, became the oldest 100 metres champion ever. By beating the top American sprinters in the IAAF Golden Sprints and the World Cup the next year he did, however, prove that he was truly worthy of the gold. A late starter, he only concentrated on sprinting at 24, and won six Commonwealth Games medals. He was coached by his wife, Margot, also a Commonwealth Games sprinter.

CAMERON SHARP

Another of Scotland's top sprinters, the former Shettleston Harrier's major championship career began in 1978 when he teamed up with Allan Wells, David Jenkins and Drew McMaster to win Commonwealth relay gold for Scotland and set a UK record. At the 1980 Moscow Olympics Sharp reached both the 100 and 200 metres semi-finals and helped Britain to fourth in the relay. His superb physique has helped him overcome a horrific car crash in 1991 which left him seriously disabled. Of his struggle he remarked, "I feel that getting out of a wheelchair, and walking unaided, was as great a personal triumph as the Commonwealth and European medals I won on the track."

SHA 16

LIZ McCOLGAN

Liz McColgan is perhaps the most remarkable distance-running talent ever produced in these islands. The single-minded determination that has seen her win two Commonwealth Golds and one World Championship at 10,000 metres can be seen in this characteristic shot, the wiry form and bunches, grinding towards victory. She has overcome a succession of injuries to keep herself at the forefront of world athletics. She never managed Olympic gold but took silver at the 1988 Olympics in Seoul. This multiple world record breaker on the road and track intends to continue running marathons – she won her first attempt in New York in 1991 and has also won in London and Tokyo.

SHA 17

YVONNE MURRAY

World indoor and European outdoor champion at 3,000 metres, Yvonne Murray sent patriotic pride soaring with a magnificent victory in the 10,000 metres at the 1994 Vancouver Commonwealth Games. As Herald columnist Jack Webster remembers it, "Wrapped in the Saltire of Scotland and weeping tears of joy, she had enough left for a memorable lap of honour which raised a deep sense of gratitude that we can produce human beings of this quality." Murray intends to defend her Commonwealth 10,000 metres title in 1998 but will in future concentrate on marathons.

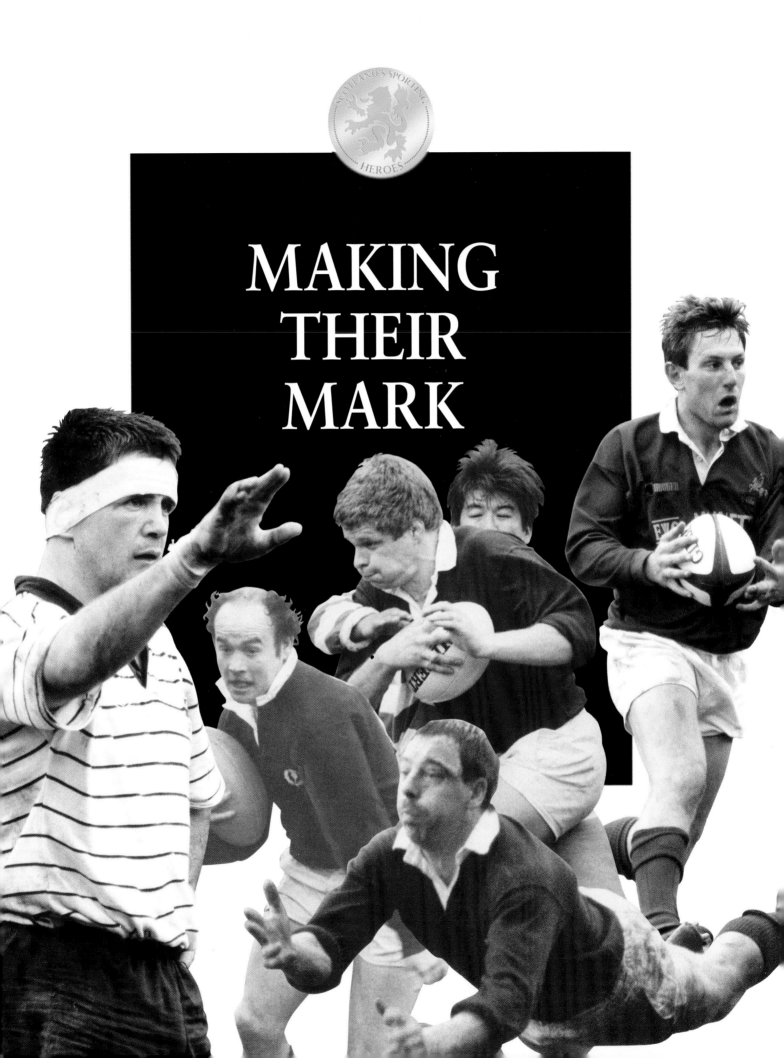

MAKING THEIR MARK

SHR 1

JOCK BEATTIE

Beattie, from Hawick, was famous in his home town for practising his lineout jumping against lamp posts in the main street, much to the consternation of local townsfolk. It paid off, however, as Beattie, one of the most respected Scottish forwards of his generation, won 23 caps between 1929 and 1936.

WILSON SHAW

Wilson Shaw was captain of the 1938 Scottish side which won the Triple Crown, a feat not repeated for more than 40 years. Shaw, who was captain and fly-half, a position now known as stand-off, scored a winning try in the last minute of the match against England at Twickenham, reckoned to be one of the best tries ever seen.

DERRICK GRANT

Derrick Grant, another famous Hawick player, was capped at wing forward in the mid 60s and played for the British Lions. On retiring he coached the Scottish forwards with distinction, including a memorable 33–6 win over England, still a record defeat of the Auld Enemy. The Thursday night before the game the side went to see the Sylvester Stallone film *Rambo*, and Grant exhorted his troops to employ similar tactics in the game. It worked.

SHR 2

SHR 3

SHR 4

GORDON WADDELL

Seen here passing in a Scottish match against France in 1962, Waddell had a short international career from 1957–62. He played with Glasgow Accies, London Scottish and Cambridge and went to South Africa with the British Lions in 1962. He moved to South Africa permanently when he married into the Oppenheimer diamond mining family, and despite a marriage break-up he remains at the helm of the business.

ARTHUR SMITH

Smith played for Cambridge University, Gosforth, Ebbw Vale and Edinburgh Wanderers. He was capped between 1955 and 1962. Arthur was a very elegant runner and went with the British Lions to South Africa in 1962. Hamish Kemp, who became SRU President, is in the background in this typical training ground shot.

SHR 5

SHR 6

HUGH McLEOD

One of Scotland's most rugged prop forwards, Hawick's Hugh McLeod is said to have had a favourite trick of picking up a handful of grass and mud which was thrust in opponents' faces on packing down in scrums. Capped between 1954 and 1962, and for the Lions in Australia and New Zealand in 1959, McLeod was a typically rumbustuous Border battler.

SHR 7

NAIRN MacEWAN

Nairn 'Splash' MacEwan – so named for a perceived lack of desire to buy a post-match drink for his team mates – once broke his jaw playing for Scotland against England. With his jaw wired he was sent back on the plane north with a pair of pliers in case he was sick, but MacEwan had the necessary toughness to overcome such niceties. That toughness was emphasised by his desire to get to the top as a wing forward when he used to drive six hours to attend training in Galashiels from his home in Inverness. He coached Scotland on retiring from active service, and played bagpipe music while handing out tartan scarves in an attempt to further motivate his players.

JIM TELFER

Jim Telfer's career has been littered with high points. Most recent was as forwards coach to the victorious 1997 Lions in South Africa. As an uncompromising number eight he played for both Scotland and the Lions. A hard man with a soft centre he single-handedly designed a style of play that helped Scotland win two Grand Slams in six years, in 1984 and 1990. Telfer had a fearsome reputation as a coach, and could reduce grown men to quivering wrecks, especially in team talks, with cleverly emphasised words. On being asked by Gavin Hastings if he could practise re-start kicks, Telfer said he didn't like teams that had to kick off more than once in each game!

SHR 8

SHR 9

KEN SCOTLAND

Ken Scotland played for Heriot's, Cambridge University and Leicester and was capped between 1957 and 1965. One of Scotland's most elegant full-backs, he was a safe handler and successful goal kicker and always a distinctive figure on the field.

MIKE CAMPBELL-LAMERTON

One of the many London Scottish stars who graced the international team, Mike Campbell-Lamerton is seen here (with the ball) on a typical bustling charge in an international trial match. He also played for the Army and was capped for Scotland between 1961 and 1966 and for the Lions on two tours – South Africa in 1962 and Australia/New Zealand in 1966.

ALASTAIR McHARG

Another London Scottish stalwart, who played for West of Scotland before moving south. Always a flamboyant figure on the field, McHarg could fill in any position on the back five of the pack and was notable in open play.

SHR 14

BILL DICKINSON (above)

In reality Scotland's first coach, although at the time he was appointed as an "adviser to the international team". Quiet, thoughtful, intelligent – he was first given the job in the early 1970s, not long after taking Jordanhill to their only Scottish club championship success. He has been very influential in the development of Scottish rugby.

IAN McLAUCHLAN (below)

Ian McLauchlan earned the nickname 'Mighty Mouse' with his tough play at loosehead prop for Scotland and the British Lions. A key member of the 1974 Lions who beat South Africa, McLauchlan's hardness was typified as an active member of the Lions '99' call – which meant the side getting its retaliation in first – and a famous occasion when he took the field against England with a hairline fracture in his leg.

SHR 18

GORDON BROWN

Always 'Broon frae Troon' the West of Scotland lock forward was one of Scotland's most prolific winners of Lions' caps, appearing eight times against New Zealand and South Africa from 1971 until 1977. He was first capped by Scotland in 1969 and last appeared for his country seven years later. Like his West of Scotland club mate, McHarg, Brown gained a reputation for his outstanding play in the loose. He was famously waved away by his brother Peter in a match with England when the elder brother thought Gordon was trying to kiss him in celebration of a successful kick.

SHR 12

PETER BROWN

Peter Brown was an explosive number eight forward for West of Scotland and Gala who was capped and captained the side between 1964 and 1973. Brother of Gordon, Peter was famous for his ungainly approach to the ball in goal kicking duties. His stay in the side, however, was not permanent. Brother Gordon once phoned him: "Great news, I have been picked for Scotland," said Gordon. "Really, who's out?" asked Peter. "You are!" replied Gordon.

COLIN DEANS

A typical pose with Deans ready to hold off the opposition. The Hawick man was capped between 1978 and 1987 and is still Scotland's most experienced hooker with 52 international appearances. Deans toured with the British Lions but was unlucky not to be capped in New Zealand.

SHR 22

ANDY IRVINE

One of Scotland's most famous and flamboyant full-backs heads towards another memorable try against Wales. Capped often by Scotland and the Lions he now has a back-up role with the SRU. A brilliant runner, he was superb in attack, though this could cause a few defensive headaches from time to time. Three times a Lion (74, 77 and 80) he was also Scotland's most capped full-back until his record was eclipsed by Gavin Hastings.

SHR 23

SANDY CARMICHAEL

The powerful West of Scotland prop-forward in a determined charge holding off a Watsonian opponent. Carmichael formed a powerful front row partnership with Ian McLauchlan both for Scotland and for the Lions. He travelled with the Lions but was not capped. When his playing career was over he became coach at West of Scotland. Carmichael is patron of the Shetland rugby club, and was a school 200 metre sprint champion. He had to come home from the 1977 Lions Tour of New Zealand after having been the subject of attacks by Canterbury players.

SHR 30

A FAMOUS THREESOME

Iain Milne (left) and John Beattie back up John Rutherford as he heads for the French line to score Scotland's first try at Murrayfield in 1980. The Scots eventually won 22-14. All three were immensely impressive club players, Beattie with Glasgow Accies, Milne with Heriot's and Rutherford with Selkirk. Milne's nickname was 'The Bear', and all three played for the 1983 British Lions.

SHR 25

JIM RENWICK

Seen here looking to thread his way through England's defence in the 1980 Calcutta Cup match watched by the respective captains, Scotland's Mike Biggar and England's Bill Beaumont. The nippy little Hawick centre was capped regularly between 1972 and 1984 and toured with the Lions in South Africa in 1980. Renwick has an impish sense of humour and a neat line in cowboy songs which made him somewhat of a cult figure on the 1980 Lions tour. His singing hero was Matt Munro, and on a chance meeting in South Africa Renwick and Munro locked themselves in the lift late of an evening and went through the crooner's repertoire.

SHR 15

IAN McGEECHAN AND SCOTT HASTINGS

McGeechan (left) although a useful centre for English club Headingley and Scotland throughout the 1970s – playing for the Lions in South Africa in 1974 and New Zealand in 1977 – he made his name as coach/manager of both Scotland and the Lions. He guided the Lions to success in the 1997 tour of South Africa. He is pictured here discussing tactics with Scott Hastings, a tough-tackling centre who became Scotland's most capped player in 1996 when he turned out against New Zealand to surpass his brother's record of 61 caps. He also toured with the Lions in 1989 and 1993.

SHR 26

SEAN LINEEN

A Scotland hero who could have been an All Black hero had he stayed in his birthplace, New Zealand. Lineen qualified by having a Scottish grandmother who did us a favour as Sean soon became a Murrayfield favourite. He played for Boroughmuir and ended his international career in 1992. Keen to make a good impression when visiting Stornoway, birthplace of his grandmother, he consulted a Gaelic friend for some words of greeting. On arrival he kissed the tarmac and proceeded, in blissful ignorance, to utter Gaelic obscenities in front of the locals. Lineen is now a successful writer and broadcaster.

ROY LAIDLAW

A perfect example of Laidlaw in action clearing the ball from the scrum against Ireland in 1988. The Jedforest scrum-half was capped 47 times for Scotland between 1980 and 1988 and formed an outstanding half-back partnership with John Rutherford at district and international level. During the height of his amateur rugby career Laidlaw was an electrician in Jedburgh, and the town contributed to his costs for the Lions tour in 1983. But even heroes have to pay their dues. On the Monday morning after helping Scotland to their 1984 Grand Slam Laidlaw was to be found fitting light bulbs to Jedburgh's public toilets.

SHR 19

PETER DODS

A Gala full-back who had a tremendous record as a goal kicker for his club and for Scotland between 1983 and 1991. Dods was a prominent member of the Gala side who won the Scottish Club Championship three times between 1979 and 1983. His goal kicking helped secure the 1984 Grand Slam, despite only being able to see with one eye after facial damage sustained during the game with France.

FINLAY CALDER (opposite page)

A group of the 1986 Japanese side try to stop Finlay Calder, a task somewhat beyond them. The Stewarts Melville FP flanker was first capped that year but made his mark in 1990 when he helped Scotland to their third Grand Slam success. Calder also toured with the Lions in 1989 to Australia, six years after his elder brother Jim had gone with them to New Zealand. In the 1987 World Cup Calder was incensed at All Black winger John Kirwan singing "Cheerio, cheerio" as the All Blacks knocked Scotland out of the competition. Twelve months later Calder found himself up against Kirwan in a sevens tournament in Australia. As Kirwan lay on the ground after a tackle Calder went in with venom. "That's a bit late mate!" exclaimed Kirwan in pain. "About a year too late!" was Calder's reply.

SHR 20

KEITH ROBERTSON

A Melrose man capped for Scotland at centre and then wing three-quarter between 1978 and 1989. Robertson was a jinky runner and frequently set up try scoring chances for club and country.

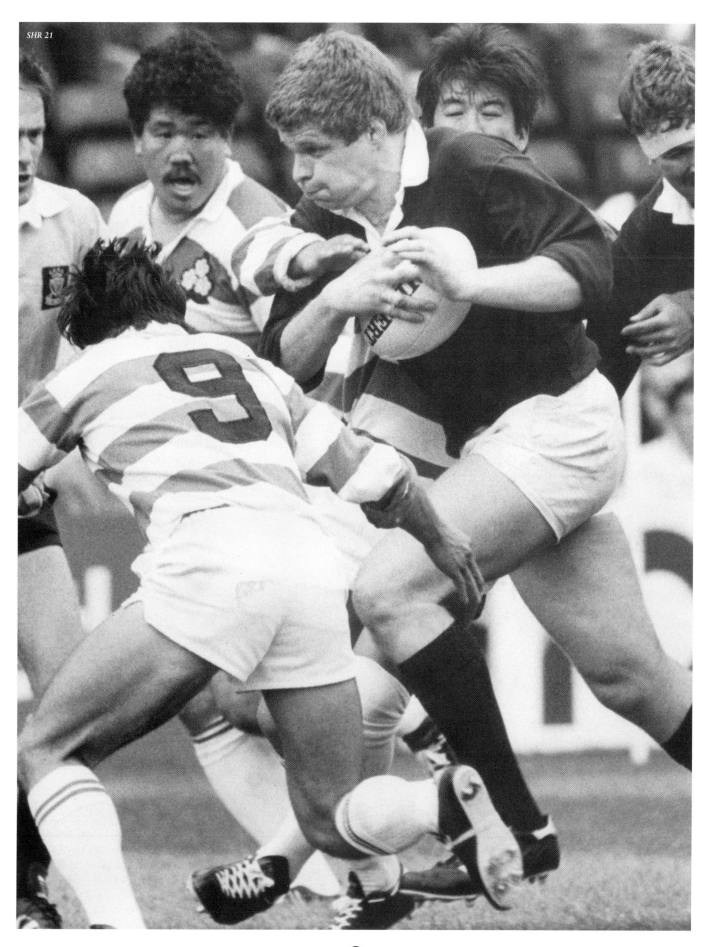

SHR 27

SHR 28

CRAIG CHALMERS

A drop-goal specialist here scoring against England in 1993. The Melrose stand-off is useful both in kicking and in opening out the Scottish attack cheered on by his big Borders following. Chalmers' recent international career has been blighted by injury.

GARY ARMSTRONG

The Jedforest scrum-half's international partnership with Craig Chalmers has frequently been interrupted because of injury. But nothing can erase the memory of spectacular individual tries in a Scotland jersey. Armstrong is a quiet man, whose love of horses is as great as his love of rugby.

SHR 29

DAVID SOLE

Never to be forgotten as the captain of Scotland's Grand Slam team which won against the odds beating England at Murrayfield in 1990. No one who was there can forget the way he led the Scottish underdogs onto the field with a slow, purposeful, menacing walk, rather than the usual trot. The cocky English were distinctly unsettled and the Scots followed up with a game played throughout with enormous vigour, surviving a last-minute English onslaught for a mighty victory. Sole played club rugby with Edinburgh Accies and also distinguished himself in 1989 in Australia with the Lions.

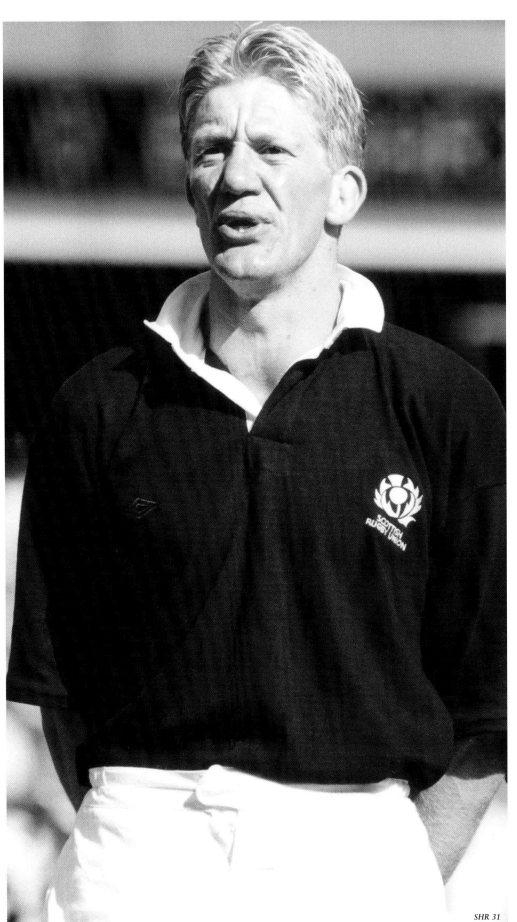

SHR 31

JOHN JEFFREY

Another real Border stalwart, John Jeffrey made a major impression in the Grand Slam team of 1990. Apart from heroics on the field he is also remembered for high jinks with the Calcutta Cup in an after-match celebration in an Edinburgh street! The epitome of the Borders rugby man, Jeffrey never played at less than 100 per cent. JJ went by the name of the 'White Shark' because of his shock of blond hair. A sheep and potato farmer in his beloved Kelso, he is now a national selector.

GAVIN HASTINGS
(opposite page)

Perhaps the most famous rugby Scot of recent years. Capped more than 60 times, Hastings also holds the record for goal kicking in internationals. His kicking prowess was turned to good effect at the end of his rugby career when he played for The Claymores, Scotland's American Football team. Gavin Hastings made his debut in 1986, alongside his brother Scott, and promptly contributed to the Scottish side's defeat of France by scoring all of his team's points with six kicks. Like his brother Scott he is one of life's enthusiasts, and after a rogue tomato hit the chief executive of one of the SRU's major sponsors at a post-match function the Hastings brothers kept a wall of silence over which one was to blame, a mystery which remains today.

SHR 33

BILL McLAREN

Never capped, illness ended McLaren's promising playing career in the Borders but this Hawick school teacher is still a true hero of Scottish rugby. A legend worldwide as a top BBC commentator with a deep knowledge of the game and its personalities, McLaren (the Voice of Rugby) was always remarkably even-handed, even in the most fiercely competitive games involving Scotland. A stickler for high standards, he deprecated unsporting behaviour whether on the park or on the terraces – the booing of an opponent lining up to take a penalty kick was beyond the pale! He was also a powerful proponent of the game at grass roots level upwards and the infectious enthusiasm which characterised his invariably informed commentaries was instrumental in raising wider interest in the sport. A national institution, McLaren is an unforgettable part of Scotland's rugby history and undoubtedly deserves a place among the eclectic bunch of personalities who can claim the status of sporting hero.